Reconceive

New thinking for progressive leaders to
create productive, positively viewed
service organisations

DAVID JOYCE | TIM BANNER

First published 2022 for David Joyce and Tim Banner

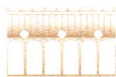

LONGUEVILLE
MEDIA

Longueville Media Pty Ltd
PO Box 205
Haberfield NSW 2045 Australia
www.longmedia.com.au
info@longmedia.com.au

ISBN: 978-0-6451742-6-7

WHAT OTHERS ARE SAYING

66 This is a thinking thing. It starts with unlearning. Everything you currently think you know, just park it, reserve judgement, and unpack those myths and unpack your assumptions. Once your thinking changes, even a little bit, there is a point of no return. There reaches a point where you actually can't go back. It is completely transformational, both personally and also for your organisation.

Renato Mota, Chief Executive Officer, Insignia Financial

66 In an age where service is quickly becoming the only differentiator amongst competitors, reconceiving service, leadership, and culture drives advocacy by delivering what actually matters to a customer. By designing and managing work in a truly customer-centric way, it challenges the way an organisation works, including leadership and culture, at all levels. Reconceive taught me to unlearn the way I had worked for nearly two decades. The things I was recognised and rewarded for as a leader in the past were challenged. Once you unlearn, you cannot go back.

Anna Leibel, Non-Executive Director Ambulance Victoria, Non-Executive Director Alfred Health, Director, Secure Board

66 How does real transformation happen? It happens by thinking about the purpose of a business from the perspective of its customers, then working on ensuring that all activity, processes, thinking, and ultimately leadership is focused on meeting that purpose. It goes to the very roots of the organisation and its leadership and their principles and thinking. It's inspiring to see the outcomes and their effect on customers, employees and the organisation itself – they are actually transformative.

Andrew Todd, Chief Technology Officer, Iress

66 Through reconceiving work, leadership and culture, our people are redesigning their own work. Their methods are being liberated, and with incredible results in terms of increased value for actual court users. They are really thinking about the people who are coming through our court who really need to resolve a matter. They are seriously energised. You're teaching people to think differently. Once the staff get into this, they love it. The judges are engaged and happy; the results really resonate with them. We have seen incredible results: time saved, convenience, usability, and registry staff focused on getting an outcome with court users rather than transacting for an output.

Fiona Chamberlain, Chief Operating Officer, Court Services Victoria

66 I like the way this approach teaches our people to study the work, use better measurement, and identify and reduce failure demand as a priority. It starts with a better understanding rather than rushing off to implement even more technology which all too often only adds to the problem. I am keen to encourage this way of understanding and improving work. It's an important evolution to improving customer value and teaches us all a lot about how our organisations work today and how that current approach is often unhelpful.

Patrick Eltridge, Chief Operations Officer, Nationwide Building Society, Non Executive Director, NHS Digital

66 This is about gaining a different perspective and a way of looking at things. It's a mindset, method, and way of thinking rather than a handbook. As a progressive leader, this resonated immediately: the need to completely rethink how you do things rather than tinker around the edges. There's real merit in thinking differently in terms of value to the customer and how you actually design your organisational systems to deliver

that value. Thinking differently about service, leadership and culture helped me drive service improvement and lower costs, and at the same time, bring more meaning and colour to the working lives of my team. What more could I ask for? This has built my capability as a leader.

Steven Leach, General Manager Operations, Vision Super

66 This challenges old-world thinking and allows us as leaders to truly empower our people to drive new and better ways to deliver what matters to customers, by encouraging challenges to current organisational systems and rules and by providing role clarity and leadership that truly supports the team to drive changes that make a difference. It shakes the foundations of management thinking, which drives effective leadership. This has helped me to deliver improved service for our customers at lower cost and improved satisfaction within the operation.

Joe Zahra, General Manager, Operations, UniSuper

66 This approach has helped us look at the way we do IT and re-orientate it back to the customer. In doing so, we have been able to strip away all of the waste, theatre, rituals and internally focused, opinion-based decision making from our work.

Rob Butera, Head of Investment Infrastructure Engineering, Iress

IS THIS BOOK FOR YOU?

It is important to acknowledge that we each see the world through our own personal lens, and this, in turn, reflects the way each of us processes information and drives our behaviour. In organisations, there are leaders who are comfortable with the assumption that all problems can be resolved by looking to the past. In other words, they assume known solutions will work in the future. They are skilled operational managers focusing on solving immediate problems and generating a much simpler representation of the complexity in which we are all embedded. They are conservative in their thinking, averse to change or innovation, and are comfortable with the status quo.

Then there are progressive leaders who are interested in change and progress. They like to think up new ways of doing things, can make sense of numerous variables interacting simultaneously, and are much more comfortable with tasks of higher complexity. They are open to new ideas and receptive to change. They can model the world in their heads, imagining what's possible, seeing things that other people cannot see, and asking themselves the question 'Why not?' These highly capable people are frustrated by the way organisations function. They question what they do and why they do it, they understand the need, and are not afraid to learn new and better ways to lead. They know that taking a 'business as usual' approach has its limitations. As Albert Einstein said, 'We cannot solve our problems with the same thinking we used when we created them'.

ARE YOU A PROGRESSIVE LEADER?

If your role in a service organisation is operational leadership, executive leadership, or as a board member, and you are: frustrated by the organisational status quo and the consequences that result, a frustration that is compounded further by the inability of traditional change approaches, fads, and magic cures to create positively viewed and productive organisations that deliver lasting improvements in service delivery, leadership, and culture; someone who actually likes, respects, and is fascinated by people, and intuitively understands that leadership is about creating social cohesion; comfortable that your role is ever-changing rather than fixed, and that your role is to support, enable, and build capability in others to work productively to their potential; and someone who still loves to learn, then this book will provide fresh thinking and opportunities on how to transform your organisation to give every customer exceptional service at less cost to the organisation. It provides valuable insights into how to build leadership capability to enable people to work more productively and create lasting positive change in people's behaviour and organisational culture.

INTRODUCTION

CONTEXT

Private, public, and voluntary organisations all provide services we either like to consume or require to lead a fulfilling and healthy life. As such, well-functioning service organisations are central to a productive and positive society. This has been a major motivation for us to write this book, as we have repeatedly seen the human and economic toll created by unproductive service organisations.

Upon studying the way services are delivered in hundreds of service organisations in the private sector, public sector, and voluntary organisations, everywhere we look, we find frustrated customers. They are frustrated by being subjected to endless waiting times on hold, being put in a queue, and long delays; being forced to interact with chatbots, apps, and websites and not being able to talk to a fellow human being because the organisation has 'gone digital'; the disappointment when something doesn't happen on time or doesn't happen at all; the despondency when being transferred or redirected to someone else or somewhere else; their raised expectations when they actually talk to the 'right' person, then having those expectations squashed when the 'right' person cannot solve their problem or lacks the authority to help; confusing correspondence, baffling instructions, and incomprehensible forms; and other internal organisational failures.

A central premise of this book is that, over time, customers come to negatively view service organisations. We have found, time and again, the failure to bring people together to achieve the purpose the organisation has been set up to accomplish is the reason customers of service organisations hold this negative view. It is not the fault of the person at the other end of the phone, email, chat window, or text message, or the fault of the person customers talk to face to face in a store, or the technician who turns up at their premises to fix, maintain, or install something, or the fault of people supporting their colleagues who serve customers, such as back-office operations, technology departments, finance, or HR. These people are trying their hardest and doing the best they can, despite the odds being stacked against them. What is encouraging is that every person we meet in a service organisation is invariably well-intended and highly motivated to deliver their best possible work, but in our experience, their efforts are undermined by the way their organisations have been set up and organised.

Conventional service organisation designs cause poor customer and employee experiences and unnecessary operational expense. They invite customers and employees to cut corners, working around 'red tape' so they can get things done. The result is an obstructive and clumsy design that wastes time and energy and frustrates customers and employees alike. Regrettably, this has manifested itself in poor service delivery, higher costs, and the creation of mental health and well-being issues for employees working within service organisations.

Our experience has shown us that customers of any service organisation want their circumstances, needs and issues to be understood, and their specific requests resolved easily and quickly. They want value out of their interactions and time spent dealing with their service organisations.

As for employees, what they want is to work in organisations where they will be engaged in their work, where relationships are cultivated, supported and valued, where their work has meaning and purpose and results in a sense of achievement, where their personal goals are supported with a clear career direction, where there is a culture of trust and flexible work models, and where they can learn new skills to further their career.[1]

We believe that the needs of the customer and employee as expressed above should underpin the intention or purpose of the

---

1   '9 things employees expect in a workplace in 2021', Helen Tobler, SEEK Employer, Mar. 2021.

organisation. If these needs are met, then the result is a positively viewed and productive organisation.

Of course, an organisation's board of directors also has a 'need'. That is to ensure there are systems enacting the board's policies. It is, therefore, critical that organisational systems are in place to maintain purpose, so the organisation continues to be productive and positively viewed. Designing organisational systems that integrate the needs of customers, employees and boards, is the work undertaken by the leadership within the organisation. The board holds the Chief Executive (CEO) to account for the quality of their work. Further, the CEO needs to ensure that the organisation achieves its intent (purpose) in a way that is acceptable to society at large. Clearly, in the majority of organisations, the leadership responsibility does not just fall solely on the CEO's shoulders, but they are ultimately responsible for the way the organisation is structured and led. Put simply, how positive the organisation is viewed and how productive it is will depend on the quality of the leadership work.

In this book, we provide numerous examples where the purpose of an organisation has been unintentionally undermined by misinformed leadership, resulting in a negative experience for customers, employees, and board members. Our experience shows that leadership capability directly impacts the quality of services provided to customers, the work completed by employees, and how successful an organisation is in achieving purpose. We believe that leaders have been stymied, let down by a lack of coherent theory, practical methods, and leadership tools relating to structuring and leading an organisation.

There is a plethora of examples, beyond those in this book, written by journalists, researchers, analysts and experts about service organisations creating bad customer experiences and poor work environments. Bad customer and employee experiences result in problems like high costs, loss of income, damage to the brand, and high levels of absenteeism and presenteeism. The impact of negative experiences in the workplace is well documented and known to lead to high levels of employee stress and anxiety.

According to Safe Work Australia, 'Work-related mental health conditions (also known as psychological injuries) have become a major concern in Australian workplaces due to the negative impact on individual employees, and the costs associated with the long periods away from work that are typical of these claims.'[2] Safe Work Australia attributes the following factors as adversely affecting workplace mental health and well-being: poor support; poor workplace relationships; low role clarity, low recognition and reward, and poor organisational change management.[3]

Thankfully, more attention is being paid to mental health and well-being in the workplace, although we argue that reported problems are symptoms of a deeper cause. It's like seeking treatment from a doctor – a person sees a doctor because they are manifesting symptoms that indicate a problem, but if the doctor only treats the symptoms, the underlying problem can remain untreated and will continue to worsen until such time as the deeper cause is found and treated.

In our experience, the 'treatment' of an organisation exhibiting such symptoms tends to concentrate on an individual action such as charismatic leadership, coaching, resilience/mindset training, and employee engagement programs. While these tactical approaches can be helpful in coping with the immediate situation, we believe that a different approach can help address the systemic causes found in the way workplaces are structured and led.

This book is about establishing leadership designed to liberate people and organisations from stultifying systems and structures. It is about eliminating the waste caused by unclear objectives, arbitrary use of power, and the excessive levels of activity and effort (much of it unproductive) found in many organisations. In short, we help progressive leaders understand and treat systemic causes of poor customer and employee experiences, unproductive activity, and unnecessary operational expense. What results is a

---

2   'Mental health in the workplace', Safe Work Australia.

3   'Work-related psychological health and safety – A systematic approach to meeting your duties – National guidance material', Safe Work Australia, Jan 2019.

productive and positively viewed organisation, that is better for customers, better for the organisation, and better for you and your colleagues.

As you read through this book, some of what you read may sound like interesting theory, but our advice is that it is always important to ask: *would it work for you?* You may also think that if this theory is so good, why isn't everyone already doing this? The answer to that is straightforward – it requires leaders to question and challenge underlying assumptions and beliefs about human behaviour and how organisations should be led and organised.

As we describe in the book, one extremely effective way for a leader to understand and test their own assumptions and beliefs is to look at their organisation from a customer's perspective – spending a few hours seeing for themselves what happens where customers interact with the organisation, then repeating this process but doing so from an employee's perspective. Leaders are astonished when they realise the money wasted and damage inadvertently inflicted on their customers and brand. They see first-hand how the systems designed into the organisation drive unexpected behaviour, cause immense frustration, create excessive levels of non-productive activity and effort (cost), and hamstring their colleagues from working effectively. The good news is that they also quickly see the opportunity for improvement, with stunning cost reductions and exceptional service delivery improvements suddenly made visible. In this book, you will hear other progressive leaders recount their experience of this experiential learning and the amazing results they have achieved.

PURPOSE

The purpose of this book is to help you, as a progressive leader, to positively change your service organisation for the benefit of all. The book is presented in two parts.

Part one is a collection of thought-provoking articles and essays on where the purpose of an organisation has been unintentionally undermined by misinformed leadership and unproductive organisation, resulting in negative experiences for customers and employees.

Each of these articles and essays may challenge your current view. The issues we highlight, may resonate or disturb. You are not alone. Progressive leaders are often frustrated by the organisational status quo and the consequences that result, a frustration that is compounded further by the inability of traditional change approaches, fads, and magic cures to create positively viewed and productive organisations that deliver lasting improvements in service delivery, leadership, and culture.

The second part of this book offers a unique approach for creating an organisation that is positively viewed by customers and employees, and how to help people come together to productively achieve the purpose the organisation has been set up to accomplish. We describe the practical methods and leadership tools for transforming your organisation to give every customer exceptional service at less cost to the organisation, building leadership capability to enable people to work more productively and create lasting positive change in people's behaviour and organisational culture. The award-winning practical methods and leadership tools that we describe in part two are based upon a coherent and integrated theory of organisational behaviour about how to lead and organise service organisations, underpinned by over 25 years of research and application in the field.

So often, in books and journals on organisational theory, we see extensive use of jargon, but without any clear definition of the terms used. Critical terms such as leader, manager, culture, authority, and even work itself are not defined but simply used, assuming a shared understanding of the definition. A **good** organisational theory uses defined terms and specifies the relationships between and among them so that clear formulations can be made and tested. To this end, we have included a glossary of terms at the end of this book.

Progressive leaders find that creating a positively viewed and productive service organisation through reconceiving and reconceptualising service delivery, leadership and culture, is hugely rewarding work. Many of these leaders have stated that once their thinking changed, it was transformational, both personally, and for their organisation, and that they will never go back to their old way of thinking. They explain how increasing their capability as a leader has been instrumental in furthering their career.

Progressive leaders in private sector organisations have been able to vastly improve customer satisfaction, retention, and sales; reduce operational expense; and improve employee engagement through creating a productive organisation that allows people to work productively to their potential. In the public sector and voluntary organisations, progressive leaders have created far simpler and better experiences for each person using a service (often at a time of great need) and, at the same time, achieve far more under constrained budgets whilst creating a more productive and sustainable work environment.

It is our aim with this book to help you, as a progressive leader, to positively change your service organisation for the benefit of all and that you are able to realise the following outcomes for you, your colleagues, your organisation, and your customers:

- A true understanding of what creates value for your customers, through learning their circumstances, needs, and issues

- Deliver exceptional services by servicing your customers through the most effective means, wherever they interact with the organisation

- Vastly improved customer satisfaction, by getting it right for your customers the first time, through designing services that are adaptable and responsive

- Colleagues who are enabled to work more productively through working in a far better and more efficient organisational design

- Reduced operational expense and increased capacity after removing failure demand and unproductive activity (cost)

- Achieve more under constrained budgets

- Managers at all levels are able, and seen, to add value to their team members

- Technology that complements human activity, enhances cognitive processes, automates simple and repetitive tasks, and further improves productive work

- Social cohesion that enables people to work productively to their potential

- Clarity for everyone about what they do, how well they are working, as an individual and as part of a team, and how they work together

- Structures that recognise work complexity to ensure everyone works on the right work, has the right authority, the right capability, and demonstrates positive behaviour

- All working relationships, hierarchical and lateral, are clearly understood and productive

- A continual and systematic understanding of shared mythologies underpinning existing organisational culture through understanding how people experience their work, their leaders, their colleagues, and the organisation

- Formation of a productive culture at all levels, through every single interaction

- Leading measures that help leaders understand how well work achieves the purpose the organisation has been set up to accomplish

- Leaders that consistently use positive leadership behaviour and symbolism to create, maintain, and improve the culture of a group of people so that they achieve objectives and continue to do so over time

- Proof of economic benefit

This unique approach to transforming an organisation is receiving recognition more broadly within the service industry, with one of our clients, WorkCover Queensland, winning the 'Australian Service Excellence Award: Customer Service Project of the Year' for continuous improvement from the Customer Service Institute of Australia (CSIA).

As a progressive leader, we hope that you find this book both stimulating and thought provoking, and that by reading the book, you are inspired to make a difference in your organisation and to society at large.

CONTENTS

PART 1
CHALLENGING ASSUMPTIONS ABOUT SERVICE, LEADERSHIP, AND CULTURE

PART 2
CREATING POSITIVELY VIEWED, PRODUCTIVE SERVICE ORGANISATIONS

CASE STUDIES WITH REAL TANGIBLE RESULTS

THE AUTHORS

DAVID JOYCE

David has worked in a variety of organisations as a senior leader, ranging from start-ups through to multinationals.

In the early 2000s David became a pioneer of, and major contributor to, the Agile, Lean, and Systems Thinking movements. This led him to being awarded the Lean Brickell Key award in 2010 and in becoming a fellow of the Global Lean Society in 2012.

Today, David is a leading authority on organisational change. He provides fresh thinking for progressive leaders, helping them to improve digital and service delivery, leadership, and culture.

David is recognised as a thought leader and is a well-known international public speaker. He is the author of the book *Theories of Work: Origins of the Design and Management of Work* and his blog has been ranked as one of the world's top 100 organisational change blogs.

TIM BANNER

Tim has consulted extensively in the public and private sectors in Australia and New Zealand. Previously, Tim spent 20 years in the UK within the Financial Services industry, and during that time he held various leadership roles.

Tim's background includes leading change in a range of organisations, from large multinationals to local government departments. Tim has helped to lead organisations to massive improvements in service, efficiency, revenue, and morale.

Reconceive

DIGITAL & SERVICE

Give every customer exceptional service
at less cost

Reconceive

LEADERSHIP

Build capability to enable people
to work productively

Reconceive

CULTURE

Create positive behaviour
and a productive culture

PART 1
CHALLENGING
ASSUMPTIONS ABOUT
SERVICE, LEADERSHIP,
AND CULTURE

1
ARE WE JUST DIGITISING 19TH CENTURY INNOVATIONS?

The management philosophy that underpins much of how we work today is Taylorism, named after the American engineer who developed the Principles of Scientific Management in the late 1800s and early 1900s. Despite having such a big influence on the world of work, very few people have heard of him.

Taylor is known as the Father of Scientific Management. He proposed that by optimising, simplifying, and automating jobs, productivity would increase. Taylor introduced an incredible range of then revolutionary management practices.

Some may sound familiar, such as:

- the separation of decision making (managers decide; workers do)

- breaking tasks down and standardising them

- time and motion studies

- creating precise processes and procedures to complete tasks

- worker training

- benchmarking and setting targets

- best practices (what he called the 'one best way')

- forecasting and planning (working closely with Henry Gantt, creator of the Gantt chart)

- quality through inspection and checking

- change by experts

- staff suggestion schemes

Taylor focused on productivity and output and wasn't concerned about worker motivation or job satisfaction. His belief was that all workers were inherently lazy and motivated by money, so he advocated the idea of 'a fair day's pay for a fair day's work'.

He was a mechanical engineer by trade, and this was reflected in his mechanistic approach to work – treating workers as machines or objects. He would time workers with a stopwatch, using the fittest and strongest man as a benchmark, and then expect other workers to achieve the same levels of productivity. If they didn't achieve the targets, they lost pay or were replaced.

In the Industrial Age, Taylor became the world's first management consultant.[4] His Principles of Scientific Management were extremely popular, spreading around the globe. Throughout the 1900s, Taylorism grew to become the dominant approach to design and manage work.

You might be thinking it's interesting to learn the root of these practices, but surely we have long since moved on from Taylorism. In today's organisations, we have far more focus on the welfare of an employee; there are policies in place to ensure people are not treated like machines, and through the creation of Human Resources and People and Culture functions, employees are no longer subject to stultifying systems and structures.

Let's examine whether this is indeed true – has Taylorism been relegated to history, or are his principles and practices still in use today? Three specific Taylor-based approaches have been chosen to test this hypothesis: process improvement, replacing workers with machines, and monitoring employees.

PROCESS IMPROVEMENT

In many organisations there have been many attempts to improve performance by using process improvement and/or 'journey mapping'. Leaders start a process improvement initiative either through recognition that the organisation either has overly complicated existing labyrinthine processes or no formalised processes at all. The thinking is that employees will perform better when following clear processes. To create better processes, leaders often turn to process improvement specialists (what Taylor called 'organisation and methods' experts).

What ensues is the mapping of current steps involved in work and, just as in Taylor's day, time-and-motion studies performed on each step, and attempts made to create simplified 'target

---

4   *The Puritan Gift: Triumph, Collapse and Revival of an American Dream*, Kenneth Hopper & William Hopper, I. B. Tauris, 2007, p. 74.

state' processes. For large organisations with many divisions, business units, and functions, 'process leaders' are often employed and process frameworks adopted. Key 'customer and employee journeys' that stretch horizontally across an organisation are defined. The aim of all of this is to define clearly understood processes with a single point of accountability attached to each in the form of a senior manager ('process leader'). As in Taylor's day, each key process is treated as a separate production line. Each process aims to deliver standardised solutions that deliver the 'optimal' outcome.

Once created and digitised into workflow software, new processes are deployed, which employees are trained to use. The usage of the new 'best practice' processes is monitored for effectiveness, often involving further time-and-motion studies and technology, an example of classic Industrial Age thinking that wouldn't have been out of place in the early 1900s.

Sadly, simply improving processes never works very well. New processes are put in place, but things don't work as anticipated, so 'workarounds' are put in place (often involving technology), adding more steps into the process each time. This continues until such a point where someone comes up with an 'idea' to improve and simplify the processes again, and the cycle restarts. Repeated process improvement is undertaken, but it doesn't improve anything in the long term.

We have seen organisations invest millions of dollars (sometimes hundreds of millions) on process improvement with little to no effect, but that has not stopped organisations from continuing down this path. Taylor's practice of process improvement is certainly still a feature of the current workplace, but what about his drive to replace workers through mechanisation?

REPLACING WORKERS WITH MACHINES: ARTIFICIAL INTELLIGENCE (AI)

Once processes are in place, tools are often employed to further automate steps within the process to achieve additional efficiency and further reduce costs (i.e., no need for people to do them). In Taylor's time, this was about adding physical tools, implements, and machines. Today, it is about automation through technology.

This thinking is becoming more prevalent with the advent of artificial intelligence and intelligent automation. Replacing 'costly' workers with robots to improve economic efficiency is a Taylorist dream. Taylor called his Principles of Scientific Management a mental revolution. The AI revolution, as it is called today, is here, and the race to employ AI is on.

It is likely that there will be many benefits from AI, however, as ever, it depends on how the technology is employed and the principles in use behind it.

The AI automation logic is leading organisations to think further about removing humans from interacting with customers and replacing them with robots. The difficulty with pursuing this approach is that customers are already frustrated at the lack of interaction they have with human beings in their service organisations. They lament on social media and crowd support sites that they cannot find a service organisation's phone number to talk to someone. They complain that they must be a 'VIP' customer or a 'Business' customer to be able to speak to a human. When they do eventually find the phone number to talk to someone, customers are frustrated that they are held in queues with long waiting times (a tactic used to encourage them to use digital channels to self-serve) and complain that, while waiting in queues, they must endure repeated messages such as 'We are experiencing long wait times. Did you know you can download our app or visit our website to [do what you want to do]?' (another tactic used to encourage customers to self-serve).

THE AI REVOLUTION!   I'M BETTER THAN A HUMAN BEING!   DOWNLOAD THE APP OR VISIT OUR WEBSITE!   I CAN SAVE YOU FOUR MINUTES PER INTERACTION!

Chatbots are just one particular example of AI that has caught the attention of leaders. Juniper Research reports: 'Chatbots hold the potential one day to replace the tasks of many human workers with AI (Artificial Intelligence) programs sophisticated enough to hold fluent conversations with human users'.[5] Juniper quoted appealing cost and time savings from using chatbots: '[A]verage time savings of just over 4 minutes per [chatbot] enquiry, equating to average cost savings in the range of $0.50–$0.70 per interaction' when compared with traditional call centres.[6]

These kinds of numbers gain management's attention. Saving four minutes per enquiry and equating that to cost savings is direct evidence of a Tayloristic approach still in use today.

Chatbots may seem appealing; however, is anyone thinking about the customer on the other end of these bots? Is anyone looking at the true systemic economics of these 'savings'? Or are they focusing, as Taylor did, on unit productivity and unit cost? There are plenty of examples that show, once the bots are deployed, the anticipated savings on the bottom line don't appear, leaving leaders confused as to why not.

ROBO-DEBT FAILURE

ACTUALLY ... I CAN ONLY USE RULES AND ALGORITHMS.

---

5   'Chatbot Conversations to deliver $8 billion in Cost savings by 2022', Juniper

6   'Chatbots, A game changer for banking & healthcare, saving $8 billion annually by 2022', Juniper Research, 9 May 2017.

In Australia, the government commissioned a computer program to recover debt, called the Online Compliance Intervention. The IT software was designed to check the income and benefits an employee was entitled to, matched what their employer had reported to the tax office. Prior to the implementation of this technology, a human being would do some investigation work and would follow up with people via letter and phone. This work was replaced by a robot that would do some checks and send out letters.

In a Media Release, The Minister for Human Services reported: 'The new online compliance system, which became fully operational in July, is now initiating 20,000 compliance interventions a week – a jump from 20,000 a year previously. Over 3 years it is expected to carry out 1.7 million compliance interventions.'[7]

Sounds fantastic. The robot seems far more productive than the humans. However, thousands of recipients of debt recovery notices were later found to owe less or even nothing.[8] 'Robodebt', as it has become known, is infamous for the great financial and emotional angst it caused many Australians, as well as incredible damage to the credibility of the Australian government. It led to a class action and resulted in a settlement worth $1.8bn between the commonwealth and victims of the scheme.[9]

Not all customers want to talk to a chatbot. When we worked in a large insurance company, we met the person who designed and implemented 'conversational chatbot' solutions, which aimed to provide 'human-like' conversational experiences for customers. Within the chatbot conversation flow was the option to automatically transfer the customer to a human being. This option was buried deep within the flow. When we asked why the option to speak to a human being wasn't offered at the start of

---

7   'New technology helps raise $4.5 million in welfare debts a day', The Hon Alan Tudge MP, #NotMyDebt, 5 Dec 2016.

8   'Centrelink's 'deeply flawed' robo-debt to face new investigation', *The Guardian*, Australian Associated Press, 13 Jun 2018.

9   'Robodebt: court approves $1.8bn settlement for victims of government's 'shameful' failure', *The Guardian*, Luke Henriques-Gomes, 11 Jun 2021.

the conversation, the answer from the designer was that everyone would use it!

In their article titled, 'Why your call center is only getting noisier', McKinsey & Company highlights the issues that organisations face after deploying various technologies which were supposed to reduce costs and improve service but failed at both: 'These technologies begin with websites, chat bots, and apps and extend to artificial-intelligence robots that simulate human conversations – redefining the way organizations interact with customers – as well as more tried-and-tested functionalities such as improved web, app, or self-service capabilities in interactive voice-response (IVR) systems. And yet, despite this plethora of technology solutions, we see that calls are not going away and instead are catching call-center executives off guard in their efforts to reduce volumes … in many instances, we've also observed that the volumes of unwanted calls exceed what would be expected during a learning period, or remain constant or rise over time, defeating strategic goals and leaving managers bewildered and unable to tie tech investments to improved operational outcomes.'[10]

For the foreseeable future, AI can only be a set of rules and algorithms. We don't even fully understand how the human brain works yet, let alone create true artificial intelligence to try and replicate it. As reported in *Wired* – 'Why Artificial Intelligence Is Not Like Your Brain – Yet': '[T]hese systems have only a few million "neurons," which are really just nodes with some input/output connections. That's puny compared to the 100 billion genuine neurons in your cranium. Read it and weep, Alexa! We're talking 100 trillion synapses.'[11]

Senior leaders often espouse that they want their organisations to be innovative, continually improve, and be differentiated on service. However, once rules and algorithms are codified, and processes are locked into technology concrete, the ability to

---

10   'Why your call center is only getting noisier', Maurice Hage Obeid, Kevin Neher, and Greg Phalin, McKinsey & Company Marketing & Sales, *Our Insights*, July 2017.

11   'Why Artificial Intelligence Is Not Like Your Brain – Yet', Lee Simmons, *Wired*, 3 Jan 2018.

innovate and improve will be inhibited and sometimes nullified. If poor service design is robotised, quality of service will go down, customers will suffer, and costs will rise as failure demand (see chapter 11, Failure demand – The invisible expense) pours in. So, while Taylor may have dreamt of replacing people with machines, the reality of doing so has been proven to be flawed in a service context.

This brings us to the third of the Taylorisms – Surveilling and monitoring employees.

MONITORING EMPLOYEES

Taylor's view of employees was that they were naturally lazy and shirkers. To ensure they did not shirk, and to increase productivity, he devised various methods to monitor their work and output. This often involved the technology of the time, for example, stopwatches, clipboards, and time-and-motion studies. Workers were monitored to ensure they met the standard times and received incentives for exceeding them.

In the *Guardian* article 'Robots have already taken over our work, but they're made of flesh and bone', Brett Frischmann and Evan Selinger state: 'The modern, digital version of Taylorism is more powerful than he could have ever imagined, and more dehumanising than his early critics could have predicted. Technological innovations have made it increasingly easy for managers to quickly and cheaply collect, process, evaluate and act upon massive amounts of information. ... When the guiding assumption of management is that employees won't be productive unless forced to be by constant observation, it engineers low morale and pushes people to act like resources that need to be micromanaged. Too often, we become what we're expected to be.[12]

---

12 'Robots have already taken over our work, but they're made of flesh and bone', Brett Frischmann and Evan Selinger, *The Guardian*, 25 Sep 2017.

Surveilling and monitoring employees is on the increase – organisations are using sophisticated surveillance systems to monitor employees and make sure they are always productive. It is now common for technology to sit in the background, collecting data on what employees are doing. Technology tracks, for example, if employees are doing their work within the specified times; how many work items are in their queue, how long phone calls take, how much time is spent on non-work activity such as surfing the web or on social media, how many emails or instant messaging chats they send, and how much work they did that day. For field service workers, the technology tracks items such as how long they took to get to a job, how long they spent on a job, how long they spent on their breaks, and how many jobs they do per day. This data is collated and reviewed by managers and teams of specialists. The consequences for morale and attrition are dire.

Since the COVID-19 pandemic forced many employees to work from home, the situation has only worsened. As reported in the *Guardian* article 'Shirking from home? Staff feel the heat as bosses ramp up remote surveillance': 'For many, one of the silver linings of lockdown was the shift to remote working: a chance to avoid the crushing commute, supermarket meal deals and an overbearing boss breathing down your neck. But as the Covid crisis continues, and more and more employers postpone or cancel plans for a return to the office, some managers are deploying increasing levels of surveillance in an attempt to recreate the oversight of the office at home.'[13]

The ABC reported in the article 'Employee monitoring software surges as companies send staff home': 'For an increasing number of Australian workers, it is now the norm to have every movement tracked: what websites you visit; how long you spend on social media; how many keystrokes you do each minute and even when you go to the bathroom. Sales of software that monitors employees working remotely have surged since the coronavirus pandemic was declared, with some companies reporting a 300 per cent increase in customers in Australia.'[14]

In the *Guardian* article 'Missing from desk: AI webcam raises remote surveillance concerns': '[H]ome workers will have an AI-enabled webcam added to their computers that recognises their face, tags their location and scans for "breaches" of rules at random points during a shift. These include an "unknown person" detected at the desk via the facial recognition software, "missing from desk", "detecting an idle user" and "unauthorised mobile phone usage".'[15]

Personnel Today reported in the article 'PwC facial recognition tool criticised for home working privacy invasion' that 'PwC has come under fire for the development of a facial recognition tool that logs when employees are absent from their computer screens while they work from home. The technology, which is being developed specifically for financial institutions, recognises

---

13   'Shirking from home? Staff feel the heat as bosses ramp up remote surveillance', *The Guardian*, Alex Hern, 27 Sep 2020.

14   'Employee monitoring software surges as companies send staff home', ABC News, Patrick Wood, 22 May 2020.

15   '"Missing from desk": AI webcam raises remote surveillance concerns', *The Guardian*, Peter Walker, 27 Mar 2021.

the faces of workers via their computer's webcam and requires them to provide a written reason for any absences, including toilet breaks.'[16]

COVID-19 has led to what's being dubbed The Great Resignation.[17] In research conducted by Microsoft, the article 'The Next Great Disruption Is Hybrid Work—Are We Ready?' reported that 'over 40 percent of the global workforce [are] considering leaving their employer'.[18] "The movement of talent is so significant and so sharp that it's different to probably anything we've seen in living memory," behavioural scientist Aaron McEwan, from global research and advisory firm Gartner, told ABC RN's This Working Life. "Today, employees don't want to be seen as workers. They want to be seen as complex human beings with rich, full lives," Mr McEwan said.[19]

Taylor's view was wrong. People aren't naturally lazy or shirkers. They don't need to be surveilled and monitored. If leaders continue down the path set by Taylor, then the inevitable result will be more people joining The Great Resignation.

---

16   'PwC facial recognition tool criticised for home working privacy invasion', Personnel Today, Ashleigh Webber, 16 Jun 2020.

17   'Buckle up, The Great Resignation is heading Australia's way', This Working Life with Lisa Leong, ABC Radio National, 13 Sep 2021.

18   'The Next Great Disruption Is Hybrid Work—Are We Ready?', The Work Trend Index, Microsoft, 22 Mar 2021.

19   'Here comes the Great Resignation. Why millions of employees could quit their jobs post-pandemic', ABC Radio National, Lisa Leong with Monique Ross and Maria Tickle for This Working Life, 24 Sep 2021.

DIGITAL TAYLORISM

In recent times a new term has entered the English lexicon: digital Taylorism. This term is the modern version of Taylorism. It takes Taylor's concepts to new levels through the use of technology, as we've explored in the three preceding sections.

The New York Times published an article about Amazon, with the headline 'Inside Amazon: Wrestling Big Ideas in a Bruising Workplace': 'In Amazon warehouses, employees are monitored by sophisticated electronic systems to ensure they are packing enough boxes every hour … in its offices, Amazon uses a self-reinforcing set of management, data and psychological tools to spur its tens of thousands of white-collar employees to do more and more.'[20]

The Economist featured a piece on the article claiming that it had struck a chord with workers across a range of different organisations: '[T]he article attracted more than 5,800 online comments, a record for a *Times* article, and a remarkable number of commenters

---

20　'Inside Amazon: Wrestling Big Ideas in a Bruising Workplace', Jodi Kantor and David Streitfeld, *The New York Times*, 15 Aug 2015.

claimed that their employers had adopted similar policies … digital Taylorism looks set to be a more powerful force than its analogue predecessor. The prominent technology firms that set the tone for much of the business world are embracing it. … The onward march of technology is producing ever more sophisticated ways of measuring and monitoring human resources.'[21]

Over 100 years after their inception, the legacies of Taylorism are not only still in use but are flourishing.

PEOPLE ARE NOT MACHINES

Taylor operated on a misguided assumption that people can be treated as machines. But an organisation that treats its people like machines, by obsessively managing people's activity and constraining people with rules and regulations that contradict common sense and a sense of fairness, will inhibit its ability to meet the purpose the organisation has been set up to accomplish.

It can easily be experienced as hypocritical when the leadership extols vision and mission statements about the apparent value of people, customers, and being the chosen supplier/employer when, at the same time, people are treated as objects.

People have an advantage over machines: they take into account purpose, and they can adapt and change in furtherance of that purpose as conditions change. The distinction between people and object relations may seem very simple and obvious. However, despite this simplicity, we all sometimes muddle them up. We have heard leaders describe people as units (of labour), resources, or numbers. Treating people in this way may not even be deliberate, but it has the effect of objectification. It can be comforting for the leadership to assume the people–object relationship because it gives the illusion that people can be controlled. We can control objects; we can only influence people. Treating people as objects breeds cynicism and malicious compliance.

---

21 'Digital Taylorism', Schumpeter, *The Economist*, 10 Sep 2015.

The irony is that attempts to control people completely are essentially self-defeating. Not only is there a question of morality but the energy required to maintain such a controlling regime will not, over time, produce an efficient outcome since, by definition, it stifles initiative, creativity, and enthusiasm. The energy put into control will exceed the energy produced from the 'controlled' person or group.

Research undertaken by SEEK has concluded that employees want to work in organisations where they will be engaged in their work; relationships are cultivated, supported, and valued; their work has meaning and purpose, and results in a sense of achievement; their personal goals are supported with a clear career direction; there is a culture of trust and flexible work models; and they can learn new skills to further their career.[22]

Digital Taylorism – treating people as machines or objects to be controlled – is the complete opposite of what employees are looking for. The importance of the employee's perspective is gaining in relevance too, with increasing skill shortages and competing demand for talented workers. SEEK reports: 'As Australia continues to grapple with COVID-19, employers across key industries are experiencing a new level of demand for workers. The competition for talent in these areas can be tough.'[23]

The impact of these factors for organisations is that if they are to have successful futures, they need to leave Taylorism behind and focus on creating attractive, productive, and positively viewed places to work. As we describe in part two of this book, the starting point is to understand not only what 'the organisation' needs but also what people need, and what they assess as worthy or unworthy. Only then can leaders be really effective in introducing change and begin building a positively viewed organisation that brings people together to productively achieve the purpose the organisation has been set up to accomplish.

22　'9 things employees expect in a workplace in 2021', Helen Tobler, SEEK Employer, Mar. 2021

23　'Australia's top 20 most-needed workers', SEEK Employment Trends, Susan Muldowney, Aug 2020.

2
WHY ARE TECHNOLOGY DEPARTMENTS SO EXPENSIVE?

Back in the 1990s, computers were becoming an integral part of organisational life. There were small teams of IT professionals working within a limited set of roles: people who specified and planned what technology to build or buy, people who built or installed it, people who tested it, and people who supported it. Specify; plan; build/install; test; and support. Simple.

Today, there is a huge variety of distinct roles involved in the specification, planning, building, installing, testing, and support of technology. To name a few: Business Analysts, Security Specialists, Database Administrators, Architects, Software Testers, Test Automation Specialists, Front-end Designers, Front-end and Back-end Developers, Full Stack Developers, Web Administrators, IT Support Analysts, Network Administrators, Desktop Support Specialists, Help Desk Specialists, and Systems Administrators.

Within each of these distinct roles lies a range of specialisations. For example, under the umbrella of a Developer role, there could be Java Developers, .NET Developers, iOS Developers, Android Developers, JavaScript Developers, and the like. Equally, there may be polyglot developers who have mastered multiple software languages.

There is also a growing field of new auxiliary roles. These include: Product Managers, Product Owners, Data Scientists, Statistical Modellers, SEO and SEM Specialists, Content Specialists, Editors, Digital Strategists, Customer Journey Champions, and Customer Experience Specialists.

There are yet more specialised jobs whose purpose is to 'uplift capability in staff' and 'ready them for the technology change', usually referred to as Change Managers, Communication Managers, Change Champions, Relationship Managers, Organisational Development Specialists, and Learning and Development Specialists.

Of course, there are the various management roles that oversee technology delivery, such as Scrum Masters, Iteration Managers, Delivery Leads, Project Managers, Program Managers, IT Managers, Heads of Technology, Chief Technology Officers, Chief Information Officers, and Chief Digital Officers.

Lastly, there is a particularly specialised role: the 'expert', or as it is often termed today, the 'coach'. Coaches work alongside teams and leaders and either specialise in methodology, for example, a Scrum Coach, or, because of their seniority, operate as an Enterprise Agile Coach.

The number of people, professions, and specialised roles involved in technology delivery is staggering. Huge budgets are consumed; the larger the organisation, the larger the spend, be it in-house, outsourced, or a combination. It's not uncommon for the technology department to be the most costly and largest department in an organisation.

IS THERE AN ALTERNATIVE TO ENDLESSLY 'FEEDING THE BEAST'?

Technology departments are clearly a large organisational 'beast', and such a large 'beast' needs to be fed, but how? Well, it is commonplace for large backlogs of features and projects to exist, and when backlogs begin to run dry, more ideas and suggestions are requested to restock the backlog again – a continuous cycle to feed that insatiable appetite.

For many organisations, this system is usually fraught with delays, capacity constraints, prioritisation issues, and growing backlogs of features and projects waiting their turn. Upfront and ongoing investment is needed for technology and teams, with large numbers of people who painfully piece together the many components of the end-to-end delivery system.[24]

The following real-life case study is a compelling example of how to break the feeding cycle and, instead, create a technology

---

24 'Connected Agile® for agile organisations', TomorrowX.

department that adds real value to the organisation's services and bottom line.

A newly hired Chief Information Officer had been asked by the board to reduce the cost and improve the productivity of the organisation's technology department. The same had been asked of the previous person in the role, but the opposite had happened: costs had risen and productivity decreased. The new CIO was as disturbed by the high operating costs and reduction in productivity of their department as the board and wanted to do something about it.

The CIO went about trying to understand the reasons for the high cost and reduced productivity. He hired a customer experience consulting firm to run a variety of workshops to gather and consolidate information. The consultants worked with newly formed cross-functional working groups who were asked to identify the 'what' and 'why' of the technology department, conducted one-on-one interview research, journey mapped existing delivery processes, voted on pain points that caused costs and inefficiencies, and provided recommendations.

The maps, illustrations, and other visualisation posters were placed on walls in a specially dedicated 'visualisation room'. The purpose of the visualisation room was to enable visitors to see how everything depicted fitted together, and would 'speed up communication and decision-making' around the need to consolidate and reduce technology spend and increase productivity. The maps and other visual aids were stunning and beautifully crafted. Any low-level detail was abstracted into the form of pictorial illustrations.

The consultants suggested to the CIO that he bring his leadership team to the visualisation room, where they could be walked through the various journey maps, posters, and illustrations, with the expected result being one of epiphany through 'moments of truth' which would subsequently lead to agreement that improvement was needed.

The leadership team went to the visualisation room and were duly walked through the journey maps, posters, and illustrations.

Each leader thanked the team and the consultants for their hard work in creating a 'wonderful looking room', and then went about denying what they had seen and simply ignored and cast aside the data. As a result, after their visit, nothing changed.

Perplexed, the CIO contacted us and asked for help. We suggested the door of the visualisation room be locked. We explained that it is pointless having a rational debate about the high cost of technology departments and any inefficiencies. There will always be convincing arguments made as to why the high costs need to be maintained and why things are the way they are. Instead of trying an approach to convince or explain, we suggested a more effective approach to changing behaviour would be to design an experiential learning session for the leadership team. The CIO agreed, and we began work with the CIO and the leadership team.

For the first stage of their learning process, they selected an innocuous and simple change from the backlog to use for learning: The contact centre agents had asked that the font and colour of a key field on their customer administration software be changed to 'bold' and 'red' respectively – a simple change. The logic behind the request was also straightforward – this field was the first field the agent used to look up a customer's details, and these changes would make it easy to find it when they switched screens, saving them time.

The request for the simple font change was made by the contact centre manager to their IT business partner (another role), who wrote it up as a request, and submitted it into the technology department backlog for estimation and prioritisation. Several weeks later, the IT business partner came back to the contact centre manager with a quote; it would cost several hundred thousand dollars to implement. The contact centre manager said that, when she read this, she almost fell off her chair.

We took the leadership team into their operation to follow the work from the original contact centre manager request through all of the people involved, and ending with the IT business partner in the technology department who had emailed the quote. This learning process revealed the reasons for the high costs for such a simple change.

There were a cacophony of actors: it had to be analysed by a business analyst for cost vs benefit; defined by a technical analyst; designed by a user experience designer; written up into a testable requirement by a specialist; approved by an architect; added to a backlog of requirements by an administrator; submitted for approval by another administrator; approved by a project board; scheduled into a plan by a project manager; approved by a program manager; allocated to a team by a resource manager; designed, built, and unit tested by a cross-functional development team; usability, accessibility, and integration tested by a team of testing specialists; added to the automated test suite by an automation specialist; approved by a change advisory board; scheduled for release by the release manager; regression tested, load tested, and security tested by various specialists; scheduled for deployment by the deployment manager; added to change logs and deployed by the deployment team; version notes updated by the technical writers; and training materials updated by trainers and champions.

They were all professionals in their field, with every person doing 'their bit', and everyone entirely disconnected from the reality of what mattered to their contact centre colleagues, or how each other worked in the operation. Each person logged their estimated time to complete their part of the work in the internal time logging application, with the bill for delivery and the timeline for implementation increasing with each addition.

The CIO and leaders learned that even simple changes came with lengthy timelines and large bills due to the various parties involved 'clipping their ticket'. It was a shock. No one had any idea what was involved in the operation – and this was for a simple change. They followed several other changes, each with varying complexity, and each were found to consume huge amounts of resource and cost.

By getting the CIO and leaders to learn first-hand what was happening, we helped give the leadership team a different frame of reference. They were able to look at the work being done with a fresh perspective, challenging their previously held beliefs and assumptions.

We then asked the leadership team to review features and projects in the technology backlog portfolio. There was a slew of features and projects queued in the backlog. Each member of the leadership team took several items and went to speak with their business colleagues who had requested the technology be built. The purpose of each discussion was to understand how each requester had determined the benefits of each of the proposed technology solutions. They were interested to understand how each item would help improve service for customers, enable colleagues to be more productive, and/or reduce costs. They also wanted to understand how the benefits would be measured.

It soon became obvious that the majority of the 'benefits' had been built on foundations of sand and should have been filed in the science fiction section. Most of the so-called benefits had either been assumed or pulled out of the air. Many items claimed the same benefits as others; for example, full-time employee (FTE) savings. When the assumed FTE savings in one area were totalled, there would have been no one left working in that department!

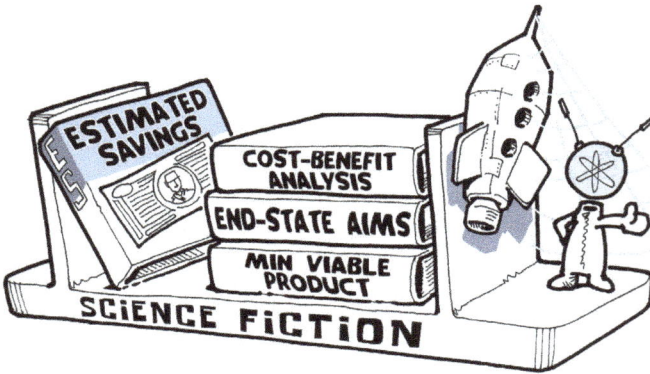

They also learnt that if a project had been allocated a large budget, a heap of other unrelated items from the backlog became attached to the project. These technology 'barnacles' were items that had previously had difficulty achieving funding on their own and were therefore destined to languish in the backlog forever. There were targets and Service Level Agreements between the technology department and their business sponsors around the length of time items were sat in a queue, so such items were increasing the average time it took for backlog items to be completed. The 'fix' was to sneak these unallocated items into large funded project work to 'get them done' to help meet the targets and SLAs. The leaders saw first-hand how this approach consumed resources and costs while yielding little benefit.

One leader commented:

> 66 *I went through it the first time, and I admit, I was in denial. I had to go through the process a few times. After the first time, I still had lots of projects in my portfolio. After the second time, I had halved that number. After the third time, only a*

few projects remained. I couldn't believe how much work was being done or planned that was of no value. The focus was on keeping everyone busy and just doing stuff.

Following this learning exercise, we asked the leadership team to spend some time in the contact centre. The organisation had recently purchased and deployed a cloud-based customer relationship management (CRM) service. The purpose of their time in the contact centre was to understand how well technology was enabling the contact centre agents to serve customers.

As part of the rollout of the new CRM, the organisation had to migrate customers from the previous CRM into the new one. The migration had taken over a year and had consumed millions of dollars in budget. If you were a customer whose account had been migrated, all was good, however, thousands of customer accounts hadn't been migrated and were left in what had been termed the 'legacy' CRM.

To confuse things further, some customers who had multiple accounts sometimes would have one account in the old CRM and another in the new. Whenever a customer contacted the organisation, there were different screens and different scripts in each CRM for the customer support agents to follow, depending on in which CRM the customer's account resided.

During each interaction with the customer, the agent had to try to determine if the customer was 'old' or 'new'. The time to serve the customer increased while this was worked out: 'Could you hold on while I just try and find your account?', the agent would say. To get the service they wanted, customers worked out how to get around the technology. When a call was answered by an agent, members of the leadership team discovered that over 60 per cent of the time a customer would have learnt to immediately say 'I am a legacy customer!' The organisation had conditioned their customers to work around the technology issues to be dealt with more efficiently.

This experience confused the leadership team. They had read reports that the new CRM implementation had been a success. We suggested they investigate by following the journey these reports had taken from where they originated, through the various levels of the organisation.

What they found was that while the purpose of the new CRM was to assist the agents in providing a better service to customers, unfortunately, the opposite was true. The front-line leaders had written reports detailing various issues, which made their way through the hierarchy. However, the reported issues had never reached the technology leadership team. Instead, the leaders received glowing reports of success; for example, 'The frontline have welcomed the new technology with open arms', and 'The customers are very happy with the improved service'. Why the disconnect? When the leadership team followed the reports through the hierarchy, they discovered that as it traversed each level of the hierarchy, the messages became narrowed and watered down. Finally, they found that when it reached the Program Management Office, one employee deleted lines that were deemed as 'unpalatable' and replaced them with 'good news' stories instead. What started off as 'It's gone in and there are significant issues' had changed to simply 'It went in'.

When asked why they did this, the Program Management Office employee stated, 'The bosses don't like bad news'. The mythology around bad news in the organisation had driven the dysfunctional behaviour and hidden the truth from the leadership team.

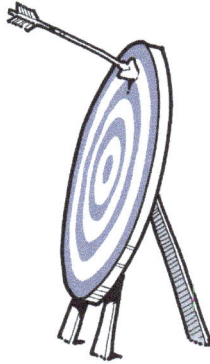

Lastly, we asked the leadership team to talk about all the targets, Service Levels Agreements, and measures used in the department. We asked them to go and see what behaviour they were driving. Here is an example of what they found:

In the Digital function, there were measures on how long customers spent on the company's website. The thinking was that the longer a customer spent on the site, the more they must be getting value from it. In response to these measures, the technologists devised ways where customers would get lost in the site trying to get what they wanted, forcing the customer to search; the more time they spent searching on the site, the better the 'time on site' numbers looked to the managers.

The number of customers who had registered for a new online portal was a measure that appeared on the executive dashboard. As the organisation had invested heavily in new digital services, it was deemed critical that the organisation's customers made use of them. After its launch, not as many customers had registered for the digital services as had been hoped. The managers in the operation became concerned that the executive, upon seeing that the number of customers using the digital service was not as expected, would start asking questions. The response was to change the contact centre scripts. Whenever a customer contacted the organisation, either through the phone or online chat, before the customer's query was dealt with, the customer would be first asked if they had registered for the new digital services. If they hadn't, they would be signed up by the agent, thus increasing the number of customers who had registered. The managers didn't care what the customer did after they had signed up, as that wasn't measured. The focus was on improving the number that appeared on the executive dashboard. The senior managers were very proud of the percentage of customers who had signed up for the new digital services, and without knowing what was really going on, the work on building the new services was regarded as a success.

As a result of each of these experiential learning experiences, the senior leaders couldn't un-see what they had seen with their own eyes or un-hear what they had heard with their own ears. One of the leaders commented:

> 66 *We have added more control and bureaucracy to 'improve' technology delivery. What I see now is that the very 'define and control' logic has caused the problem of late, expensive, and wrong technology.*

Another said:

> 66 *I now see the world differently. I've come to realise that most of my instincts on technology are deeply flawed.*

And another stated:

> 66 *We've spent millions on these IT 'solutions', but how we interact with customers is a mess. No one in the technology teams has a clue about what actually happens in the work, or what matters to customers. We've just built or installed technology based on how we think we should do it, and that has just compounded what I now see are the real issues. I've seen how they are affecting the service we give to our customers and our staff's ability to serve them.*

Resistance to simplifying and creating a more productive and less costly technology organisation was defused due to the dissonance created by each of the experiential learning sessions outlined above. The CIO and leadership team collectively agreed that a more productive organisation design was needed, and they could each see where operating costs would reduce as a result.

Examples such as these are not unique. We have seen the same, or similar, in hundreds of organisations. If you feel that your technology department is too expensive, or is not as efficient as it could be, then perhaps, as we describe in part two, the first step is for you to go through a similar experiential learning process.

3
ARE AGILE METHODOLOGIES A FAD?

Over the course of time, various methodologies to improve organisations have come and gone. Magic cures or panaceas promised to solve our problems but, instead, turned into fads and died, only to make way for the next wave of 'new thinking' and jargon. Let's investigate Agile methodologies and whether they are just another fad, or if there is a better way for organisations to achieve true agility.

WHEN DOES A METHODOLOGY TURN INTO A FAD?

A magic cure, panacea, or fad is a methodology that can be characterised using the diffusion of innovations (DOI) theory developed by E. M. Rogers.[25] The model indicates that the first group of people to embrace something new are called 'Innovators', followed by 'Early Adopters'. Next, are the 'Early Majority', followed by the 'Late Majority', and with the last group to eventually adopt termed the 'Laggards'.

Attached to each of these adopter phases are belief systems that develop around the so-called cure. For example, when a new methodology is created, the Innovators begin to use it. Next, the Early Adopters jump in, promoting the promise that this methodology is better than the last. Popularisation occurs in the Early Majority through promulgation by 'thought leaders' who write books, articles, blogs, social media posts, and present at conferences. The big consultancies then market and sell frameworks and solutions to the Late Majority, and, finally, the 'Laggards' catch up through 'fear of missing out' (FOMO).

When the purported benefits of a methodology do not materialise or cannot be sustained, it is labelled a 'fad', begins to lose favour, and eventually dies out. However, even when there are numerous, well publicised failures, there will be those who remain loyal and believe that it would have worked, but that 'people didn't do it properly'. The most common defence is to point to what has worked and ignore everything else. After all, 'It works perfectly well, if you do it right' is the defender's retort.

---

25 Diffusion of innovations, Wikipedia.

The greatest irony, though, is that as one methodology wanes, a new methodology appears to take its place – often the same methodology, but repackaged in new language. And then we are off again with Innovators, Early Adopters... We call this the Fad Lifecycle.

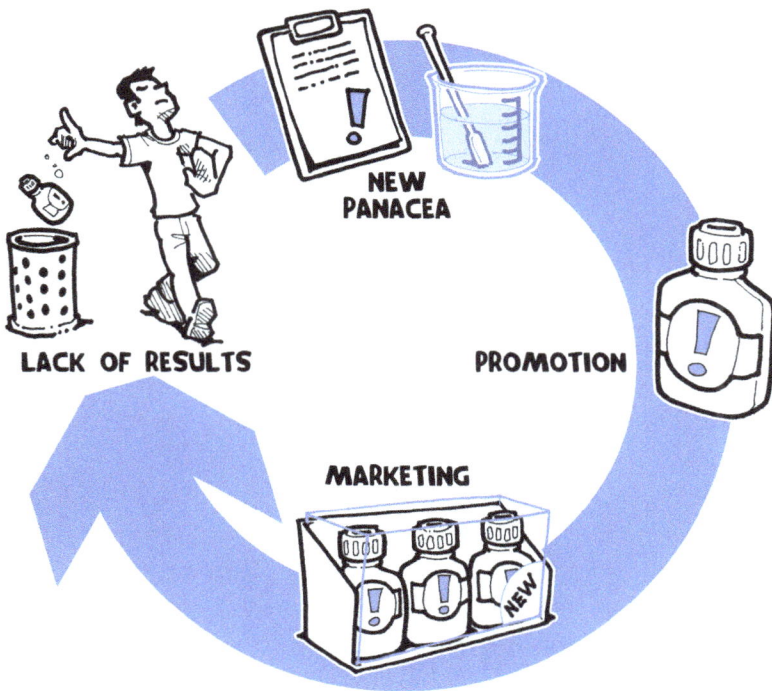

ARE AGILE METHODOLOGIES LIMITED?

If you are involved in transformation today, then you will no doubt be aware of the term Agile. Agile started as a manifesto to guide software development, but over the ensuing years it morphed into a methodology for project management. More recently, companies selling the Agile solution recommend that it should be implemented across the **entire** organisation.

Certainly, an outstanding job has been done at marketing Agile methodologies, so much so, that today, Agile is in no doubt part of the mainstream lexicon, with both the Late Majority and Laggards now embarking on transformations using 'Agile ways of working'. Agile has become trendy and is promoted as the real cure to outdated command-and-control styles of management, extending well beyond the purpose for which it was created.

Unfortunately, as we have seen through the Fad Lifecycle, popularity doesn't necessarily translate to results. Experience shows that Agile methodologies are limited in what they can do to transform organisations and are at serious risk of joining their predecessors in the long procession of failed fads. Remember Total Quality Management, Process Re-Engineering, Balanced Scorecard, Core Competencies, and Self-Directed Teams? Time has proven that they, too, were not the cure they claimed to be.

Even so, organisations have invested significant outlays on Agile transformation programs, but when these programs are studied to assess their ability to influence and create a sustained shift in organisational behaviour and leadership capability, all are found wanting.

When we work with organisations that use Agile methodologies, employees inform us that their organisation may appear agile, but they refer to it as 'putting lipstick on a pig'. They cite, for example, that they may look agile with all the trademark symbols like Post-Its on the walls, stand-up meetings, and new ways of working, but beyond this veneer, little of substance has changed.

Agile methodologies are limited. They lack the practical methods and leadership tools based on sound organisational theory required to solve the core issues that hinder true agility, such as control from above; negative mythologies underpinning culture; stultifying systems and structures; quality of leadership; unproductive behaviour and activity; and lack of clarity in role, accountability, authority, and working relationships.

Agile methodologies ignore these core issues and, instead, focus on the low-hanging fruit: the work and organisation of the work. The reason Agile methodologies fall short is the lack of a foundation in good organisational theory that addresses why people behave as they do and how to build a productive organisation. (See chapter 9, The practical value of good organisational theory.) Through the lack of practical methods and leadership tools to solve core issues, along with an absence of real knowledge and testable theory, the potential benefits from introducing Agile methodologies are predictably constrained and often not realised at all.

In light of Agile methodology transformation failures, there are those that claim that newer Agile methodologies – such as DevOps, Modern Agile, The Spotify Way, and Strategic Agility – will 'do it this time'. And here begins the first stage of the never-ending Fad Lifecycle!

MAKING THE POTENTIAL OF ORGANISATIONAL AGILITY A REALITY

Progressive leaders are aware of the fad lifecycle and the trendy nature of Agile methodologies. They recognise the limitations in these approaches. They understand that these methodologies do not create a sustained shift in organisational behaviour and leadership capability, or lead to the changes in organisational systems and structures necessary to ensure lasting improvements in their organisations.

As we describe in part two, to realise the considerable potential of an Agile organisation, there first needs to be a reconceiving of the organisation's core – one where sound organisational theory, practical methods, and leadership tools are used to create a productive organisation, which results in:

- everybody having clarity of what they do, how well they are working, as an individual and as part of a team, and what authority they have to make decisions

- productive social cohesion that enables people to work productively to their potential

- structures that recognise work complexity to ensure everyone works on the right work, has the right authority, the right capability, and demonstrates positive behaviour

- well-designed systems where everyone can use judgement and discretion and are enabled to improve the way their work is done

- technology that complements human activity, enhances cognitive processes, automates simple and repetitive tasks, and further improves productive work

- measurement systems that give insight into how well the organisation understands and delivers the things that achieve purpose

- a continual and systematic understanding of shared mythologies underpinning existing organisational culture through understanding how people experience their work, their leaders, their colleagues, and the organisation

- clear understanding of all hierarchical and lateral working relationships

- leaders that consistently use positive leadership behaviour and symbolism to create, maintain, and improve the culture of a group of people so that they achieve objectives and continue to do so over time

Our own recent experience provides a telling example of the contrast between implementing an Agile methodology versus adopting practical methods and leadership tools to create a productive organisation as described in part two. A large Australian organisation had undertaken an Agile transformation. Nearly every workspace had Post-Its on the walls, stand-up meetings were occurring daily, and the organisation had been reorganised into Squads, Chapters, Tribes and Guilds using the Spotify Model.[26] Training had been conducted throughout the organisation, and various Agile coaches had been employed to facilitate learning and improvement.

Senior leaders, however, were disappointed with the results, and we were called into the organisation to help to identify and address what wasn't working as it should be. We applied the practical methods and leadership tools we describe in part two to build leadership capability, create a productive organisation, and create lasting positive change in people's behaviour and culture. Once this organisational shift was made, the long sought after results were realised and recognised throughout the organisation as a successful transformation.

A highly regarded Agile practitioner, and one of the original authors of the Agile Manifesto, visited the organisation and was amazed by the positive impact the new productive organisational design had along with the positive resulting change in behaviour.

Through the application of new thinking in an organisation, it is finally possible to achieve true agility and break free of the Fad Lifecycle.

---

26 'Scaling Agile @ Spotify with Tribes, Squads, Chapters & Guilds', Henrik Kniberg & Anders Ivarsson, Oct 2012.

4

BEST PRACTICE – ARE COPIES AS GOOD AS THE ORIGINAL?

Often, when leaders seek to improve their organisation's performance, they look to other organisations for one that is known as a great exemplar of best practice and copy its best practice methodology, based on the underlying assumption that copying will achieve the same positive results. At first glance, this may appear a sensible approach – don't spend resources and time reinventing the wheel – after all, it worked for them, so surely it will work as well for us too! That, however, has been repeatedly proven not to be true.

Copying and importing solutions is not a new phenomenon. Since the 1970s, people have copied and installed the 'Toyota Way'. Tools used in the Toyota Production System (TPS) were copied, but the people copying these tools did not stop to ask themselves if they had the same problems to solve as Toyota. After all, these tools had been specifically created to resolve Toyota's problems, not anyone else's.

Taiichi Ohno, the man who developed the TPS, was clear that copying wouldn't provide the answers for other organisations. Instead, he advised that leaders needed to think differently about how to solve their problems: 'Unless we completely change how we think, there is a limit to what we can accomplish by continuing our same thinking. We cannot find a new path unless we take the leap and turn our awareness and our thinking upside down'.[27]

Toyota leaders suggested that copying the TPS tools was folly; it was the change in thinking behind the TPS that should be understood. History has proven Toyota leaders were right – no one attempting to copy TPS has been able to achieve the same

---

27   Ohno, Taiichi. Taiichi Ohnos Workplace Management: Special 100th Birthday Edition, p. 18, McGraw-Hill Education.

results as Toyota. The lesson was there for those who wanted to see it.

W. Edwards Deming also warned of the dangers of copying. Deming made a significant contribution to Japan's reputation for innovative, high-quality products, and for its economic power. He is regarded as having had more impact on Japanese manufacturing and business than any other individual not of Japanese heritage.[28] He warned: 'American management thinks that they can just copy from Japan—but they don't know what to copy! ... They look at examples and without theory they learn nothing. ... To copy is to invite Disaster.'[29] Just as Toyota's warnings had fallen on deaf ears, so did Deming's.

Let's fast-forward to today. We still have leaders trying to improve the way work and people are organised. Now the goal is to break down silos, reduce risk, and improve productivity, alignment, cross-collaboration, and knowledge transfer. Many models have been developed to achieve this transformation, ranging from autonomous workgroups to cross-functional teams to self-managed teams.

One of the most popular models today, which many organisations are copying – as it is regarded as best practice – is the approach taken by the music streaming service Spotify.

In 2012, Henrik Kniberg and Anders Ivarsson published a whitepaper titled 'Scaling Agile @ Spotify'. The whitepaper described a model of Squads, Tribes, Chapters, and Guilds. However, in the same way that Toyota leaders warned of the folly of copying the 'Toyota Way', Spotify leaders also warned against copying what has been termed the 'Spotify Way'.

One of Spotify's leaders was quoted in an InfoQ article, aptly titled 'Don't Copy the Spotify Model', as saying: 'The model can help you to understand how things are done at Spotify, but it is not something that you should copy in your own organization. ... The Spotify

---

28   W. Edwards Deming, Wikipedia.

29   'People Copy Examples and Wonder Why They Don't Succeed', The W. Edwards Deming Institute, Sep 2015.

model changes all the time as people at Spotify learn and discover new things. We look at what we do, we examine the problems, and solve them.'[30]

Marcin Floryan, Chapter Lead at Spotify, even quotes Toyota's Taiichi Ohno in his presentation 'There is no Spotify model': 'Stop trying to borrow wisdom and think for yourself. Face your difficulties and think and think and think and solve problems yourself.'[31]

Despite these clear warnings of the ineffectiveness of copying the Spotify Way, it has been promoted as best practice. Organisations around the globe have attempted to adopt the model into their organisations. The results of research into transformation failures,[32] detailing examples of organisations who have failed after faithfully implementing the Spotify Way, are simply ignored by those who continue to promote it as the best way forward.

---

30 'Don't Copy the Spotify Model', Ben Linders, InfoQ, Oct 2016.

31 'There is no Spotify Model', Marcin Floryan, InfoQ, 2016, slide 52.

32 For example, see 'Spotify as a role model? What you should know before you copy their organizational model', Christoph Schmiedinger, 2013; see also 'Failed #SquadGoals Spotify doesn't use "the Spotify model" and neither should you', Jeremiah Lee, Apr 2020.

So, what do progressive leaders need to do? We believe that rather than using 'Let's copy the best' as a starting point for organisational improvement, the first question needs to be 'Are we solving the same problems as the organisation we want to copy?'. In the case of Spotify, the problem they are trying to solve is to 'unlock the potential of human creativity – by giving a million creative artists the opportunity to live off their art and billions of fans the opportunity to enjoy and be inspired by it'.[33] Most likely, this is not the problem your organisation is trying to solve.

To achieve similar results to those of successful organisations like Toyota and Spotify requires exactly what Taiichi Ohno advised, to 'turn our thinking upside down' through the application of a different philosophy, tailored to meet the specific outcomes your organisation seeks to improve.

As we describe in part two, adopting practical methods and leadership tools based on sound organisational theory to create a positively viewed and productive organisation will enable you to develop a tailored solution for your organisation that ensures improved performance.

Create what will work for **your organisation**. That's a better place to start.

---

33 About Spotify, Spotify.

5
IT JUST WORKS – A CUSTOMER'S DREAM?

It just works... Those three words became synonymous with Apple. It was used over and over by Steve Jobs as he unveiled new products at Apple keynotes.[34] The sentiment behind this statement was that Apple's technology helped make customers' lives better, worked as they expected, and solved their needs, seamlessly and flawlessly.

Can this sentiment be applied to service organisations? Do our services make our lives better, work as expected, and work seamlessly and flawlessly for customers of the service? Is it true that *it just works*? Let's look at an experience I (David) had recently.

---

34   "It Just Works.", Techcrunch, MG Siegler, Jun 2011

I watch my football team religiously. What matters to me is that I can access live games so I can watch my team play. A telco had bought the rights to the football games, so in order to watch the games live, I had to take up one of the telco's products, such as buying a mobile phone plan or an internet connection package. I chose the internet connection option. I was already out of contract with my current internet service provider (ISP), so off I popped to my local telco store to make my purchase so I could start watching the games.

When I walked into the telco's store, I was greeted by a smiling employee in a bright company-branded t-shirt who had an iPad in her hands. Great, I thought, I can give her my details, and she can sign me up. When I asked her for help, I was informed that her job was to 'check me in'. 'Pardon?' I said. 'You can't just sign me up? What is the purpose of the iPad?' She told me that all she could do was take my details, tap them into the iPad, and put me in a virtual queue; where I would wait until a sales consultant could help me. It was at that point I noticed a group of other customers sitting on chairs, looking around expectantly every time a t-shirt-wearing telco employee walked past. I trudged over to join them. Checking people in and putting them in a virtual queue is a common tactic – it looks better to have people sitting on chairs than physically standing in a queue.

NEXT

Talking to my newfound seated friends, I learned that many of them had been there before. They were queuing to get things fixed, to complain, to question something they had been sent, to chase something up, or to correct issues that had occurred. In other words, the majority of people were in the store because of failure demand. (See chapter 11, Failure demand – The invisible expense.)

After a long wait, watching people in the queue slowly being led away, one by one, to see a sales consultant, it was my turn. I sat with the sales consultant, who was equally as smiley as the person who had checked me in. He asked me what I wanted. I explained that the football games were important to me, and I wanted to sign up for a new internet connection so I could access them. He checked my ID (driver's licence, recent bills, and the like) and inputted these into a computer. The computer informed us that I was eligible and that cable internet was available at my premises. BUT…

Part way through filling in the various online forms, the computer crashed, and we had to do it all again as my partially completed order had become 'stuck'. The sales consultant explained to me that this happened to him all the time. When I asked if he could fix it, he told me that he couldn't. He could only lodge a ticket for his IT help desk to fix it, and they never had.

I was then asked when I would like the installation of the new internet connection to happen. I could choose either an AM or a PM appointment, Monday to Friday. 'I work during the week; can you do a Saturday?' I asked. 'We don't like making too many weekend appointments,' I was told. After some negotiating, I was given a Saturday installation appointment – in three weeks' time. I was instructed that I had to be on the premises from 7:30 am to 12:00 pm, as the technician could arrive anytime between those hours. As everything was now booked, I waved the corporate t-shirt-wearing employee goodbye and left the store.

When I returned home, an email was waiting for me. It was from the telco, congratulating me on signing up, confirming my order details, and confirming the installation appointment date. I also received a text message with the same information.

A few days later, I received another email from the telco; 'Hello, love top-quality Sports? Would you like to sign up?'. Hadn't I already signed up? Why were they inviting me to buy the Sports package? I ignored the email, but it left me wondering how many people receive similar automated emails, which then drove them to contact their telco... The telco was good at creating their own failure demand!

The day before the Saturday installation, I received a phone call while I was at work. Answering the phone, a robot informed me that 'Your installation is booked for this Saturday, between the times of 7:30 am and 12:00 pm. Be aware that the installation could run overtime into the afternoon, so please ensure that someone over the age of 18 is present at the property at all times.' I was then asked to please press 1 to agree, or 2 if I didn't agree. The robot wouldn't allow me to ask any questions. I selected option 1.

The day of the installation arrived. I waited at home expectantly for the technician to arrive at 7:30 am. It got to 8:30 am, then 9:30 am, then 10:30 am, with no sign of anyone. Were they coming? The robot had told me that the installation could run overtime, so wouldn't they need to be here by now?

I called the contact centre, battled through the phone menu options ('press 1 for...'), and finally got through to a person, who took me through some identification security checks (including the details I had already keyed in via the phone). Before discussing my problem, the telco consultant asked me to confirm my home address, email address, if I had signed up to access their online services, and contact preferences (so she could update their CRM). She would have been driven by prompts on her screen to do this, so I gave her what she needed so we could get onto the real reason for my call. Once we got to my problem, the telco consultant stated she couldn't see any installation booking for me *(what?)*, and eventually, after some searching in *another* of the telco's databases, the consultant found my records and told me that the technician was on his way. I ignored the automated customer satisfaction survey at the end of the call. I also ignored the survey I received in both my inbox and my phone.

Around 11:30 am there was a knock at the door. The technician had arrived. 'We've got a problem,' he announced. He led me outside and pointed to the telegraph pole in front of my house. 'See that X marked on the pole?' he asked, 'That means the pole is defective. I can't attach a cable to it until the electricity company confirms that it can bear the weight.' 'But I wanted to watch the football game tonight on my TV!' I said in frustration. 'Nothing I can do, mate. I need to call the head office, and they will fill in a form to give to the electricity company, who will then advise if we can use that pole.' He brought up his iPad, filled something in, called his head office, lodged the issue, and then drove off…

Back on the phone again, I battled through the phone menu options ('press 1 for…'), through the security checks, and when I got through to a person, asked what was going on. 'Sorry', he said, 'that is now with the Installations Team'. Quoting a Service Level Agreement, he said, 'Someone from that team will call you back in the next three days'. It wasn't his fault. Despite the slogans purporting to give great customer service, the opposite was true; policies, systems, processes, and rules designed into the organisation were driving the non-productive behaviour and creating poor customer service.

I wondered why someone from the telco hadn't contacted me anytime in the prior three weeks I had been waiting for the technician to arrive to ask if there was an X on the pole outside? It is a predictable and preventable problem; however, the current organisational systems and structures had hidden these typical and predictable problems and meant they were not visible to leaders.

Two days later, I received an email (I had been 'diarised'): 'We're waiting on updates from the power company. Our Dispatch Team will be in touch within 72 hours from today.' Another Service Level Agreement satisfied; meanwhile, it was three weeks and three days and counting, with no end in sight.

I didn't hear anything after another 72 hours, so I rang the contact centre again, went through the menus and security checks, only to be told that the pole was ok and that I could book another appointment. Why hadn't they rung me and informed me? Why did I have to do all the chasing and work hard to become a customer? Didn't they want me as a customer? The answer is because that is how the organisation had been designed; various functions and specialists doing their bits to standard times, putting me back into queues and passing me around. No one was looking at the sales flows to establish if it was difficult for people to become customers. It was only because I wanted to watch the football that I persevered. So, I booked an installation for the following Saturday and was informed that the technician was scheduled to arrive anytime after 12:00 pm.

On the Saturday afternoon, a different technician to the first one arrived. He asked to come into the house. 'Where would you like the modem?' he asked. 'In the study, please, and can I have the Digital TV box connected to the TV in the lounge?' I replied. 'We don't do internal cabling,' he said, 'You need a Wi-Fi device for that, and they haven't sent you one'. Another example of a predictable, preventable problem. The telco was so busy dealing with all of the failure demand they were creating that there was no capacity to do proactive things like ensure that when a technician turned up, they had everything they might need to complete the work for the customer. The technician was perfectly capable of doing internal cabling or carrying Wi-Fi devices in their van, and yet someone somewhere in the organisation had deemed that to be an unnecessary cost that hindered productivity. The technician set to work, and after lots of clambering around the roof, drilling, and pulling wires, the internet connection and Digital TV box were installed.

'You're all done,' the technician told me. He seemed very eager to leave. When I asked why, he showed me a list of jobs on his iPad. Mine was flashing red. 'I've spent too long on this job,' he said, 'I have a lot of other jobs to do that have been scheduled for today'. The poor man was under surveillance by his own organisation.

After he left, and now that equipment was installed, I thought, let's test it. Switching on the TV, I was presented with a list of set-up instructions. Step 1 I completed ok. Step 2 I was prompted, 'Please enter your Activation Code'. Huh? What activation code?

Looking through the materials that came with the modem and Digital TV box, I found a set of instructions. Under step 2, it read, 'Please enter your Activation Code. We would have sent this to you in an email or an SMS'. I had received neither. The technician had left, and he hadn't given me his phone number, so I couldn't ask him for help. I decided to turn to Google for help.

The first Google page returned links to Crowd Support social sites with suggestions for resolution. Clicking on each of these, I was taken to the telco's Crowd Support portal, where I read through complaints from other confused telco customers who had had the same problem; they hadn't been sent an Activation Code. It was clear no one from the telco was doing root cause analysis on the various issues being discussed in their forums.

There was a range of suggestions given by customers on the Crowd Support portal, none of which worked for me when I tried them, or they were outdated – for example: 'Click on this link on their website to get the code', but when I went to the website, the link no longer existed. There were a lot of aggrieved customers commenting on the portal, some of whom expressed frustrations such as 'I wish I had never gone with this telco.' Oh no, I thought, I don't have a choice, I want to watch the football!

Exasperated, I rang the telco and plunged into their menus again and got through to yet another person. After the same identity checks again, I was asked various questions as they tried to locate my activation code. Finally, I was given the code. I completed the activation and setup, then sat down later that evening and watched a football game. THE END... Well, no, actually.

Three days later, there was a knock at the door. 'Hello, I'm an inspector from your telco. I'm here to check your installation. Unfortunately, the previous technician installed your internet wire too close to the power line, so I need to do it again.'

Really? You couldn't make this up!

Did 'It just work'?' What were the number and variety of typical, predictable, and preventable issues I ran into? (Hint: There were a lot.) What were the unnecessary operational expenses? I doubt anyone in the telco knows. They will only record costs for each part of the service, not the overall economics. (See chapter 16, Are you running your organisation through the rear-view mirror?)

There will be no line items for the costs of failure demand and unproductive activity.

What is invisible to the telco leaders is how the current obstructive and clumsy design wastes time and energy, frustrating customers and colleagues alike, and creating unnecessary operational expense.

THE WAY TO IMPROVE SERVICE

In our experience, examples such as the one above are all too common. We have seen the same or similar in all organisations that we have worked in around the world, be they private sector, public sector, or voluntary organisations. The telco is no worse or better than any other service organisation, but like many, there is room for significant improvement in their service delivery. As we describe in part two, we believe the first step to achieving that improvement is looking at the service from the customer's point of view.

When using a service, customers think of their service organisation as a single entity, not as a series of separate organisational channels or departments. All they want are their circumstances, needs, and issues understood and their specific request resolved fully, easily, and quickly. In other words, they want to derive value from their interactions and time spent dealing with the organisation.

The way to improve any service is for the leaders to learn first-hand what matters to their customers, understanding predictable circumstances, needs, and issues. Only then do leaders learn what value customers do or don't get from their services, and, most importantly, why it is that way. Leaders then see how current policies, systems, processes, and rules designed into the organisation drive non-productive behaviour, cause immense frustration, and hamstring their colleagues from effectively serving customers.

Seeing the organisation as a customer sees it shifts their starting place from thinking they know what their problems are to one where leaders discover they have, in fact, quite different problems to solve. From this starting point, what results is the creation of a positively viewed and productive organisation.

We assisted a telecommunications client to adopt this approach. They experimented with how to deliver the perfect customer experience for new internet customers.

Once the leaders studied the current design of organisational systems and structures, they were astonished at how difficult it was for people to become customers, how difficult the organisation was to deal with, and how technology had institutionalised those difficulties and locked in higher costs. They then acted to create more productive organisational systems and structures. As a result, people at all levels gained a clearer understanding of what was expected of them; they were enabled to use their full capabilities in exercising judgement and discretion in roles that freed them to work productively; a far more productive working environment was created, so each person understood where each other's authority started and finished; and technology was applied that complemented human activity, enhanced cognitive processes, and automated simple and repetitive tasks. The improvement work quickened exponentially, resulting in a reduction of 45 per cent in the average costs per order and an increase from -27 per cent to +55 per cent in their Net Promoter Score over a 14-month period.

If only they had a deal for broadcasting the football...

CUSTOMER

6
CUSTOMER EXPERIENCE
INITIATIVES – CAN THEY WORK?

Customer Experience, commonly known as CX, is everywhere. Private sector, public sector, and voluntary organisations have all embarked on CX initiatives with the aim to transform their services, empower employees, and optimise their operations.

Why? Fundamentally, it is because improving the customer experience can improve competitiveness and financial returns for an organisation. An oft-quoted Forrester Research report states that a: 'one-point increases in CX scores can translate into approximately $10M's - $100M's in annual revenue.'[35]

---

35 See, e.g., 'CMO Collaborators Fill the Gap in the C-Suite to Drive Business Growth, Accenture, Interactive Research Finds', Accenture Newsroom, 3 Oct 2018.

Despite these compelling reasons to implement CX initiatives, it seems the theory is not translating into reality for many organisations. Microsoft commissioned a study of CX projects in Australian financial services. In their findings, they found: 'More than four out of five (81 per cent) of financial organisations have had failed customer experience projects'.[36]

This is an incredibly high risk and poor return on the significant investment involved in CX initiatives. Therefore, the question becomes, given the great benefits of CX initiatives, is there a way to ensure their success? Certainly, there is plenty of advice available. Indeed, you may have heard some of these 'must do's' before:

- Create a dedicated customer driven CX team

- Focus on delighting your customers and continually listen to your customers to obtain insights

- Prioritise work on customer value from a backlog of ideas

- Ensure you map the end-to-end customer journey and remove pain points

- Break down silos across the organisation; create small cross-functional empowered and autonomous teams

- Create a safe-to-fail culture

- Be outcome driven; measure customer value and link back to business value

- Ensure single ownership of the CX initiative and instil a CX culture

---

36   'Microsoft urges financial services firms to tackle data blindspots to reduce risk of costly failed CX projects', Microsoft, Feb 2019.

All these recommendations sound great; however, the challenge is to convert these words into actions that will be embraced by the people who have to implement and work with the changes to their well-established working patterns. Every day.

Not surprisingly, the commonly adopted 'do it to people' approach to CX initiatives ends in concerted resistance within the organisation and is seen as a lamentable failure by its leaders. Why? Because initiatives that threaten underlying assumptions and beliefs that shape behaviour are simply resisted until the initiatives are judged to be a mistake, a failure, or a complete waste of time and money. (See chapter 18, A cure for that déjà vu feeling of cultural resistance.)

Today's CX initiatives lack coherent organisational theory to help guide change. (See chapter 9, The practical value of good organisational theory.) They also lack practical methods and leadership tools required to solve core organisational issues such as control from above; negative mythologies underpinning culture; stultifying systems and structures; quality of leadership; unproductive behaviour and activity; and lack of clarity in role, accountability, authority, and working relationships. Through a lack of practical methods and leadership tools to solve core issues, along with an absence of real knowledge and coherent theory, potential benefits are predictably constrained and often not realised at all.

Progressive leaders question the efficacy of today's CX initiatives, and with good reason. These initiatives lack guiding theory, practical methods, and leadership tools to unlock the profound benefits of improved customer and employee experience. As we describe in part two, when these critical and fundamental parts of the change process are adopted, when the context for improvement is driven by what creates value for customers and how best to service them, when people are organised and enabled to do that work more effectively, and when productive leadership practices are embedded, the result is a positively viewed and productive organisation. That is a successful CX initiative.

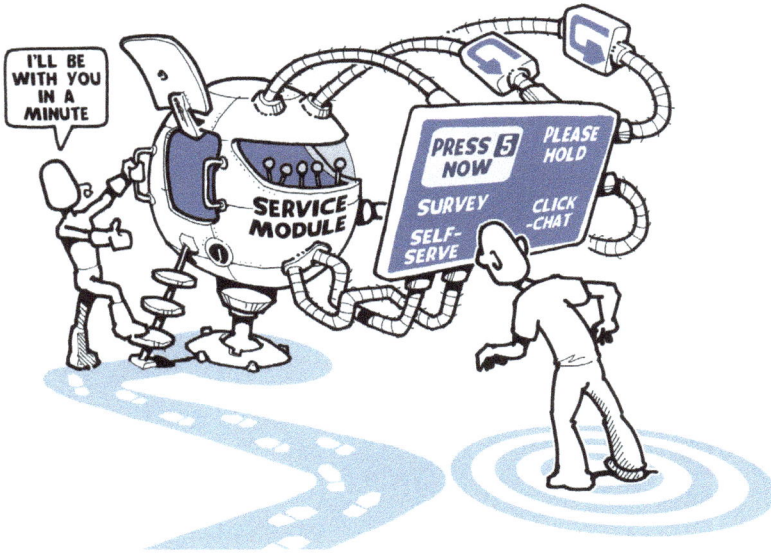

7
ALL CUSTOMERS WANT IS STUFF THAT WORKS

When organisations go through a digital transformation, they inevitably include changes to their technology tool kit. Particular focus is given to 'upgrading' customer-facing technology and technology to improve employee productivity. In both cases, it is assumed that new tools are needed. But what are the unintended consequences associated with upgrading these tools?

CUSTOMER FACING TECHNOLOGY

There is a plethora of off-the-shelf products available in the marketplace for customer-facing technology. Some of the must-have technology tools available now are:

- Assisted service

- Self service

- Automatic call routing

- Predictive dialling

- Branded online communities

- Automated electronic surveys

- Automated notification

- Display advertising

- Check-in kiosks

Those are a lot of tools for managers to choose from, people to implement, and customers to navigate – and this is just a sample of what is on offer. So, what are these tools supposed to achieve for a business? According to the sales pitch, these tools will:

- Give customers a choice on how they interact with you, seamlessly and cohesively

- Give the customer what they want, with no delays, and with less effort

- Enable customers to be easily informed of progress

- Reveal what does and doesn't work for customers, resulting in improved and streamlined processes, and

- Increase self-service to reduce your costs

Excellent! Where do I sign? Well, not so fast. Let's first check what experience has shown us.

WHICH NUMBER DO I PRESS TO GET REAL HELP?

We know that these types of tools are frequently purchased (even the local library has automated call routing, which only has two choices!), but their effectiveness at improving the customer experience is variable at best, and unfortunately, the negative views held by customers are well known: customers are irritated by 'press 1 for .....', 'please state the nature of your enquiry', and chatbots that fail to get them to someone who can help them. When they do get a real person, they have to repeat themselves, and do so every time they are passed on to yet another person in yet another section somewhere in the organisation; they are infuriated by customer service operators who follow scripts and say things like 'my computer is running slowly...' (which is the operator's code for 'I'm waiting for the computer to tell me what to say next'); they complain about constant no-reply messages or surveys; and they are annoyed at the failure to get through to a human being who can solve their problem.

What customers have been quick to learn, though, is the power of social media. Customers have learned to tweet, Facebook, or Instagram their issues and complaints as a quick way of bypassing technology that they see is failing to help them. These savvy customers have learned that their service provider will address their issues faster if they complain on social media than if they were to use the organisation's customer technology tools. It turns out they are right, as their service organisation will be worried about brand damage.

The damage to an organisation's brand can be swift and wide-ranging. As reported by news.com.au: 'The social media pages of Australia's major telcos seem to be [the] most effective way to be heard and ... [get] the quickest response time ... Visit the Facebook pages of Telstra or Optus and you'll reliably see a torrent of customer complaints in the comments section under sleek PR videos.'[37]

Increased failure demand reflected through negative comments on social media is a signal to leaders that something is not working with their services; however, the signal isn't being recognised. Instead, to deal with the increased demand, more resources are hired to join the 'social media response team'. Technology is installed to post back pre-written messages to 'buy time', 'turn negatives into positives', and give the appearance of listening to customers. The result is higher ongoing costs for the organisation and more unhappy customers, because

---

37 'This could be Australia's angriest Telstra customer', Nick Whigham, news.com.au, Jun 2017.

customers recognise glib, scripted responses. Exacerbating the negative perception by customers is the instruction they receive to take their questions 'offline'; thus, they end up back in the same flawed organisational systems they started in, with their issues still unresolved and infuriating them further. That is a very powerful negative feedback loop!

TECHNOLOGY FOR IMPROVING PRODUCTIVITY

The other component of the technology toolkit are the tools that reportedly improve productivity and reduce operational costs. Tools are purchased to manage loyalty, experience, interaction, relationships, complaints, issues, cases, workflow, documents, workforce optimisation, and knowledge management. This isn't an exhaustive list either!

The benefits expected are:

- Enable the front-line to focus on the customer

- Make the workforce more efficient and productive, with higher utilisation

- Improve morale through better skill assessment and employee coaching

- Improve forecasting and scheduling of resources – balancing work across functions

- Optimise prioritisation, routing, and queuing of work; route customers to the right area of expertise

- Automate business rules and protocols

- Receive high-quality information to enable better decision-making

- Meet business goals, targets, KPIs, and SLAs

It is no wonder managers are attracted to these kinds of tools.

MY COMPUTER SAYS NO

Customer-facing employees are not mad, bad, and/or stupid. They don't want to tell customers 'My computer says no'. They want to give good service – that's part of their original motivation to work in customer-facing areas. The problem is people who serve customers are less motivated when they work in organisational systems where they feel controlled by technology. It is common for technology to drive dysfunctional and unproductive behaviour that infuriates customers and lowers employee morale. They are unable to escape the policies, processes, and rules embedded into the IT systems. Warning lights flash if they spend too long on the phone talking to a customer; their activity is tracked and reported on; and productive working nosedives. The computer says no to them just as often as it does to customers.

A simple example is 'live chat' support. Promoted as a means to improve service, live chat is added to websites and apps to provide the facility for customers to talk directly to a service agent (rather than call the contact centre). It sounds good: click and chat to someone straight away. Unbeknown to customers, the agents at the other end have productivity measures to meet. They can only spend so much time on each chat, often using copy-and-paste pre-canned responses given to them by the computer, as well as having multiple chat windows open simultaneously so they can talk to multiple customers at the same time.

The extent to which technology is a benefit depends on how it helps or hinders the way work flows and helps customers get what they want. Problems occur because the technology is not actually dealing with what's wrong with the design of organisational systems and structures – it just reinforces those shortcomings.

HOW CAN WE GET TECHNOLOGY TO SUPPORT BETTER CUSTOMER SERVICE?

Walk into any service organisation and you will find both types of technology tools in place or being configured, installed, or upgraded. Sometimes you even find a tool is being replaced by an identical tool, this time from a different vendor. In all instances, significant financial and human resources are expended. But once installed, leaders find that these tools aren't improving the performance of the organisation or the customer experience as expected.

As Douglas Adams wrote: 'We are stuck with technology when what we really want is just stuff that works'.[38] Prior to purchasing a tool, leaders should be asking: Will this technology prove useful in my organisation, and how do I know?

---

38 *The Salmon of Doubt: Hitchhiking the Galaxy One Last Time*, Douglas Adams, William Heinemann Ltd., 2002, p. 115.

To answer this question, understanding the efficacy of the service in solving customer problems should be the starting point, not technology. The guiding principle needs to be knowledge first, technology last. Technology should complement human activity, rather than control.

What can you do differently tomorrow? We explore this in more detail in part two, but, essentially, a more effective and less costly approach is to use the following steps:

1. Determine what creates value for customers and how best to service them, and use that information to set the context for improvement

2. Organise and enable people to deliver outcomes more effectively, supported by productive organisational systems and structures

3. And only then, apply the minimum required technology that complements the more effective organisational systems and structures, enhances cognitive processes, and automates simple and repetitive tasks.

Following these three steps enables organisations to employ technology tools that can help give every customer exceptional service **at less cost** to the organisation and enable people who serve customers to work productively, to their potential.

8
TECHNOLOGY-LED CHANGE PUTS THE CART BEFORE THE HORSE

You can't move today without bumping into an article or presentation that warns of the perils of 'being Ubered', a phrase coined by Publicis Groupe CEO Maurice Levy, meaning your organisation is at risk of being disrupted, dethroned, or threatened with extinction by more advanced competitors, and that, to survive, an organisation must evolve.

These sentiments were front and centre of retiring Cisco CEO and executive chairman John Chambers' message in his final keynote speech: "'40% of businesses in this room, unfortunately, will not exist in a meaningful way in 10 years," he told the 25,000 attendees, adding, "If I'm not making you sweat, I should be."'[39]

Demise through disruption is a marketing message that technology firms have been very effective in promoting. Their

---

[39] 'Retiring Cisco CEO delivers dire prediction: 40% of companies will be dead in 10 years', Julie Bort, *Business Insider*, 2015.

premise is that the prevailing answer to disruption is to invest in technology.

It is tempting, as a business, to believe in this silver bullet solution. After all, we are promised, just install new technology and a better future is guaranteed! Certainly, technology can help complete existing processes and tasks more quickly, but does that necessarily make your services better or more competitive? And while it may make technology firms lots of money, ultimately, automation doesn't really help leaders solve core organisational issues such as control from above, negative mythologies underpinning culture, stultifying systems and structures, quality of leadership, unproductive behaviour and activity, and lack of clarity in role, accountability, authority, and working relationships.

Look around. There are no doubt people at the lower levels of the organisation who are aware of the risks of blindly following the technology-driven solution. However, if their leaders accept the technology silver bullet, these people have limited authority to influence that decision. Instead, all they can do is raise their concerns and then hunker down and focus on the process of implementation.

This technology-led approach is a classic example of a reinforcing loop. That is, an action produces a result, which influences more of the same action.[40] In other words, introduce new technology and then repeat, repeat, repeat.

Employing technology to cure all ills is not a new phenomenon. Yet, despite the evidence of repeated failure, the technology-led paradigm is still assumed to be the single best way forward.

This phenomenon has been described since people embarked on technology initiatives as a means to improve their organisations. Back in 1993, Clive Holtham wrote: 'One of the problems in discussing how to make groups more effective is that the information technology thinking driving it is rooted in traditional,

---

40   Reinforcing Loop, The Way of Systems, Gene Bellinger, 2004.

but potentially or actually inappropriate, paradigms'.[41] Although written 30 years ago, the technology-led paradigm still prevails.

So, based on these observations, what is the first step to effectively dealing with the 'demise through the disruption' mantra, if it is not technology first?

Progressive leaders know that to apply technology to already ineffective work designs predictably leads to frustration, failure, and lament, or, at best, mediocre change. In fact, what needs to change first is the way in which work is designed, organised, and managed. And, critically, this change should be customer-led, not technology-led.

Instead, as described in part two, the application of a different philosophy is required, where what creates value for customers and how best to service them sets the context for improvement, and people are organised and enabled to deliver outcomes more effectively, supported by productive organisational systems and structures. Only then can technology be applied that complements the more effective organisational systems and structures, enhances cognitive processes, and automates simple and repetitive tasks. This approach enables organisations to build long-term, sustainable, nimble, and successful businesses that are designed to adapt.

What does this more productive design look like in operation? Rob Butera, Head of Investment Infrastructure Engineering, Iress, a software company for the financial services sector, shares the approach he has found that works to create effective and positive IT changes:

> 66 *It's not surprising that much of the IT that is built isn't of value because the process of delivering IT doesn't really focus on value; it focuses on delivering things that somebody thought of, that somebody had an opinion about, and that's what the purpose becomes: deliver the thing.*

---

41   Holtham, Clive, *Improving the performance of workgroups through information technology*, City University Business School, 1993.

We've left the comfort of the IT department, and that allows us to construct real relationships with people who use our services or use the things we build, and that changes an enormous amount with regard to my decision making as an IT professional and the things that I might do. The best way to describe it is a partnership. There's a shared body of knowledge, and that body of knowledge relates back to customers, and the way customer work is done. So, whenever we talk about bringing in an IT solution for something, we are already starting off with this groundwork of knowledge around customers and customer work.

Effectively, as an IT team, we are compelled to make the IT changes at any given time that yield the most value for customers; that's what we are there to do. The customer work is central.

We try to reduce mental fatigue, to reduce cognitive load; work should just flow in. Somebody should be able to pick it up and be presented with the right information, at the right time, at the right place, to facilitate good decision making, and then make a decision, put in the decision. The mechanical work of processing should be taken care of for them.

So much of the IT that we used to build for our own people created friction: it made you work hard and put you in a bad mood; you had to fight it. We are trying to create something that does quite the opposite. Ultimately, the greatest achievement of the IT group is that we have been able to complement the more productive organisational systems which improves the work it does for customers.

Instead of a technology-led approach, let's focus on first creating a productive organisation which helps to create the conditions where people willingly work together and give their best, before we press the technology help button.

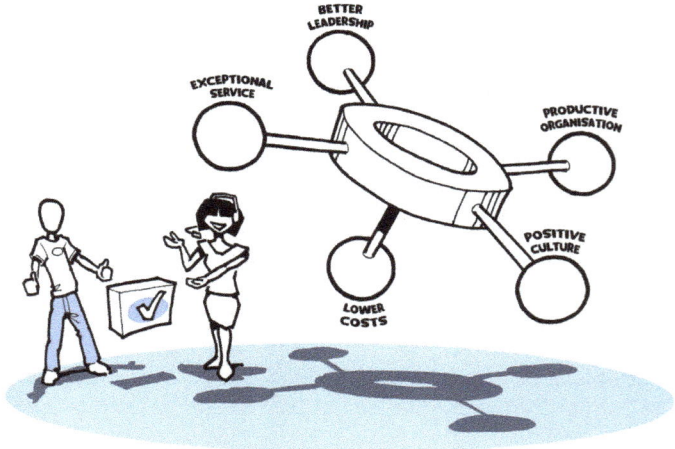

EXCEPTIONAL SERVICE

BETTER LEADERSHIP

PRODUCTIVE ORGANISATION

POSITIVE CULTURE

LOWER COSTS

PART 2
CREATING POSITIVELY VIEWED, PRODUCTIVE SERVICE ORGANISATIONS

INTRODUCTION

In part one, we presented a collection of thought-provoking articles and essays on where the purpose of an organisation has been unintentionally undermined by misinformed leadership and unproductive organisation, resulting in negative experiences for customers and employees.

Some of the articles and essays, and the issues we have highlighted, may have resonated or disturbed. You are not alone. Progressive leaders are often frustrated by the organisational status quo and the consequences that result, a frustration that is compounded further by the inability of traditional change approaches, fads, and magic cures to create positively viewed and productive organisations that deliver lasting improvements in service delivery, leadership, and culture.

The second part of this book offers a unique approach for addressing the issues described in part one. This approach draws on models from Systems Leadership (*Systems Leadership:*

Creating Positive Organisations, Macdonald, Burke and Stewart, Routledge 2018), specifically: Systems and System Design, Values and Culture, The Nature and Complexity of Work, The Work and Tools of Leadership, The Work of Team Leaders and Members, The Principles of Human Behaviour. They are all used with the authors' permission. The award-winning practical methods and leadership tools that we describe in part two are based upon a coherent and integrated theory of organisational behaviour about how to lead and organise service organisations, underpinned by over 25 years of research and application in the field. In part two, we describe how to transform your organisation to give every customer exceptional service at less cost to the organisation, build leadership capability to enable people to work more productively, and create lasting positive change in people's behaviour and organisational culture.

By applying the theory, practical methods, and leadership tools described here, in part two, progressive leaders, worldwide, have been liberating their colleagues and organisations from stultifying systems and structures, and eliminating the waste caused by unclear objectives, arbitrary use of power, and excessive levels of activity and effort (much of it unproductive) found in most organisations.

Progressive leaders find that creating a positively viewed and productive service organisation through reconceiving and reconceptualising service delivery, leadership, and culture is hugely rewarding work. Many of these leaders have stated that once their thinking changed, it was transformational, both personally and for their organisation, and that they would never go back to their old way of thinking. They explain how increasing their capability as a leader has been instrumental in furthering their career.

Progressive leaders in private sector organisations have been able to vastly improve customer satisfaction, retention, and sales; reduce operational expense; and improve employee engagement through creating a productive organisation that allows people to work productively, to their potential. In the public sector and voluntary organisations, progressive leaders have created far simpler and better experiences for each person using a service (often at a time of great need) and, at the same time, achieve far more under constrained budgets whilst creating a more productive and sustainable work environment.

This unique approach to transforming an organisation is receiving recognition more broadly within the service industry, with one of our clients, WorkCover Queensland, winning the Australian Service Excellence Award: Customer Service Project of the Year for continuous improvement from the Customer Service Institute of Australia (CSIA).

We hope that you find part two both stimulating and thought provoking, and that you are inspired to make a difference in your organisation and to society at large.

9
THE PRACTICAL VALUE OF GOOD ORGANISATIONAL THEORY

An organisation generally requires people to work together to achieve the purpose it has been set up to accomplish. Part of the challenge is that individuals bring their unique complexity to any situation, including their work. This book recognises that leadership and creating change in this context can be challenging, and requires consistency and persistence. We embrace the complexity that people bring, but we also acknowledge that to be successful in productively achieving a purpose, leaders benefit from having good theory on which to base their approach.

We described in part one the dangers of using magic cures, fads and shortcuts. It's human nature to want to know the latest quick and easy solution to everything. There are three areas of life where people seem particularly vulnerable to fads and shortcuts: dieting, parenting, and leadership.

Examining the latter, we see that many leadership theories are presented as being the silver bullet or having a secret ingredient. Basically, these are not theories at all, and could be more accurately described as magic cures. Each is short-lived, generates wasted effort, and detracts from the real work and purpose of the organisation. Our experience has shown us that organisational change is a complex matter, and approaching it without a coherent theory to guide that change is a recipe for disaster. So, if you are looking for a quick fix to create a positively viewed and productive organisation, we wish you luck. This is not the book for you.

The world is changing at an increasingly fast pace. Lack of practical methods and leadership tools to solve core issues, accompanied by an absence of real knowledge and coherent theory, impede progressive leaders from solving the problems they face today.

Significant improvement in performance can only be achieved through the adoption of new methods and leadership tools that break with those that have led to the unintentional mistakes of the past. Which leads to an important inflection point. If progressive leaders truly want to transform their organisation to become positively viewed and more productive, what is required of leaders is significantly different to what they have been conventionally taught. A better, coherent and integrated theory of organisation is required.

John Kotter's book *Leading Change* states: 'I estimate today more than 70 percent of needed change either fails to be launched ... fails to be completed ... or finishes over budget, late and with initial aspirations unmet.'[42]

Further to this, McKinsey & Company noted: 'It is no easy matter to bring about major change in a large, complex organization—whichever sector it's in. McKinsey research has found that 74 percent of private-sector transformation efforts fail

---

42   Kotter, John P., *Leading Change*, Boston, MA: Harvard Business School Press, 1996.

to meet their objectives, while in the public sector, the failure rate is even higher, at 80 percent.'[43]

There are a plethora of other similar observations written by journalists, researchers, analysts, and experts. Whatever data or quote you use, it is clear that changing any organisation is challenging and rarely goes to plan, but when the end result *is* achieved, it can be hugely rewarding for all.

WHY USE THEORY?

Some people use testable theories underpinned by years and years of research and recognise human meaning, whilst others may use theories plucked from LinkedIn or a conference presentation. Worst case scenario: people may be using no formulated theory at all. They may state that 'theory is for academics' or that they are 'more interested in doing practical things'. In other words, the person is flying by the seat of their pants.

Many capable leaders use implicit theory daily. When this is done well, they may be described as a charismatic leader with a hint of mystery or magic. There are other leaders who will argue that good leadership is just common sense and experience, which becomes highly prized over theory. We argue that all leaders use theory. It may be implicit or unformulated theory – which, by definition, is difficult to replicate or scale successfully. Even common sense is based on theory; it just happens to be implicit theory. It is assumed you either have common sense or you do not, without questioning what it is.

Ultimately, creating positively viewed and productive organisations involves changing other people's behaviour. Creating effective change needs to recognise that all people hold assumptions, beliefs, aspirations, and values. In short, this is the human dimension of change. Often, when changes are introduced

---

43 'Putting people at the heart of public-sector transformations', McKinsey & Company, Martin Checinski, Roland Dillon, Solveigh Hieronimus, and Julia Klier, Mar 2019.

into organisations, the change processes do not recognise or, worse, reject the importance of this dimension. If the human dimension of change is not recognised, then any change is at great risk of being rejected by the very people it seeks to help. (See chapter 18, A cure for that déjà vu feeling of cultural resistance.)

We, like most other people, have seen, time and again, change initiatives that never make it to implementation or fail after implementation. The prevalence of change initiative failures raises questions about the quality, or lack thereof, of any underlying theory upon which the change was based.

To be valid, a theory must explain all the activity in the field it covers, and allow users of the theory to predict outcomes under varying conditions. We argue that unsuccessful change initiatives did not have good coherent theory underpinning the intended change, and therefore are almost always likely to be rejected or suffer substantial growing pains at the practical level.

WHAT IS GOOD ORGANISATIONAL THEORY?

Instead of a rigorous and agreed set of terms and definitions, organisational theory is subject to fads and jargon. A good organisational theory uses defined terms, and specifies the relationships between and among them so that clear formulations can be made and tested. So often, in books and journals on organisational theory, we see terms not defined. Critical terms such as 'leader', 'manager', 'culture', 'authority', and even 'work' are not defined but simply used, assuming a shared understanding of the definition. To this end, we have included a glossary of terms at the end of this book.

As well as undefined terms, there are often confusing terms such as self-directed teams, flat structures and even flatarchies. Do such teams and structures have no managers or leaders? Does everyone in the team do the same work or get the same pay? How will people know what they are doing? How will people know when they are successful? The lack of a clear definition inhibits understanding of organisation and leadership and hence limits the application of any theory.

As a comparison, professionals in other fields are specific about, for example, the effect of smoking on the lungs, stress on a bridge, aerodynamic properties required to keep a plane in the sky, or the temperature in a reduction cell needed to produce aluminium. All these examples depend absolutely upon a base of shared and precise definitions of entities and the clear description of properties, relationships, and constraints for each entity. In turn, such definitions and descriptions allow a clear understanding of the relationships (or processes) that apply in given circumstances, and allow prediction of the effects of changing the parameters or constraints of those processes. In other words, the theory is well understood and can be applied across a range of scenarios, because the theory's components are defined and understood.

Whilst there is agreement in technical fields over the need for theory, definition, and clear articulation of process, it is curious that organisational behaviour and design fields remain theory deficient. Indeed, in these fields, if the ideas and concepts put forward are precise in nature, they are widely criticised for being too academic. Alternatively, ideas and concepts, regardless of merit, are considered out of date or at the end of their shelf life when a new fad appears which seems to promise something newer, better, and shinier. The implication is that an organisational theory is only allowed a specific amount of time to be relevant, regardless of its content or credibility. While this constant turnover of ideas sounds exciting, it does not further our understanding of why people behave as they do in organisations, or how to build a productive and positively viewed organisation.

REAL
KNOWLEDGE

CLEAR
CONCEPTS

TESTABLE
THEORY

DEFINITIONS

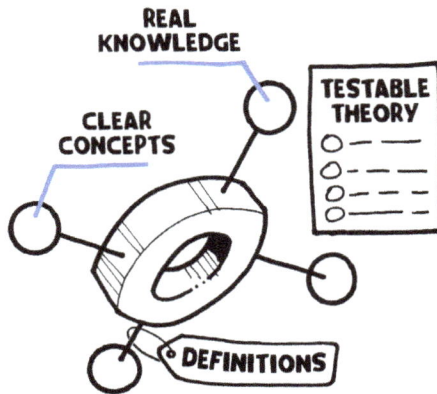

In the absence of real knowledge and testable theory, there seems to be a tacit assumption held by many that we cannot do much better than we are doing now in the leadership, management, and organisation sphere. For better or worse, they remain somewhat mysterious. We believe and argue that leadership, management, and organisation can be understood, that significant improvement is possible, and that the methods of implementation and the outcome can be predicted accurately from theory.

What progressive leaders need is better understanding of leadership processes, human behaviour, and systems and organisational design, so they can create more effective organisations to meet human, organisational, and societal needs. In the following chapters, we describe how to apply good organisational theory to help leaders move beyond magic cures, enabling organisations to deliver on all these needs.

10
BUILDING A BETTER ORGANISATION
FOR CUSTOMERS AND COLLEAGUES

It is common to hear leaders in the private sector, public sector, and voluntary organisations espouse 'Our customers are at the centre of what we do', or similar sentiment. Behind these words, the leader's intent is to build a better organisation by making services easier and better for customers. The strategy is one of transforming the organisation to become customer-centric.

Customer experience statements can be great rallying calls. However, progressive leaders recognise the problem to solve becomes: How do you ensure such slogans live and breathe within the organisation and avoid becoming just words on a corporate screensaver?

Conventionally, leaders think that if their colleagues follow the 'be customer-centric' instruction, the organisational ethos and values will change and customers will reap the benefits. This is what we refer to as the 'wave a magic wand' style of leadership! The reality, despite the prevailing rhetoric, is that customers see little evidence of their services improving, and colleagues continue to work within stultifying organisational systems and structures that prevent them from serving customers productively. Consequently, leaders become disillusioned by the various promises made by traditional change approaches, fads, and magic cures to achieve their customer-centric strategy. The result: frustration, loss of customers, and poor business outcomes.

THE HIDDEN COSTS OF CONVENTIONAL SERVICE DELIVERY

Service organisations are typically divided into separate organisational departments, or channels, delivering particular services or functions. Each has a different leader, who, in turn, has their specific targets, objectives, and budgets to meet. The assumption is that if each leader does their bit well, the whole service will improve for customers. It is a flawed assumption. In reality, people operate within individual departments or channels – there is no 'work together or collaboratively' reflected in the organisational structure. The result: poor service delivery to customers, which, in turn, leads to higher costs to the organisation.

Conventional service delivery is not designed based on how the customer wants to obtain value. The relationship norm between a customer and their service provider is usually transactional. The customer is forced to transact in a standard way, through multiple front doors, often funnelled to a channel that is assumed, by the organisation, to be cheaper to deliver.

What is invisible to leaders is that these conventional designs cause poor customer and employee experience and unnecessary operational expense. The hidden cause is restrictive red tape – policies, systems, processes, and rules that have been adopted, reviewed, and adapted over time. What results is an obstructive and clumsy design that wastes time and energy and frustrates customers and employees alike. Such designs invite customers and employees to cut corners, working around the red tape, so they can get things done.

A CUSTOMER'S PERSPECTIVE

In service organisations, there commonly exists a problem in perspective by those designing and delivering the service. People in organisations are normally inward thinking; in other words, 'What do I/we need?' They are socialised to look at work from a functional and internal perspective, viewing the organisation from the inside out. When not considering a service from a customer perspective, performance can look really good when, in fact, as we illustrated in part one, the opposite is often true.

When using a service, customers do not think of separate organisational departments or channels. Neither do they value internal organisational objectives, targets, and budgets. Customers think of their service organisation holistically, from the outside in. All they want are their circumstances, needs, and issues to be understood and their specific request resolved easily and quickly. In other words, they want to derive value from their interactions and time spent dealing with the organisation.

The starting point for giving every customer exceptional service at less cost is taking a customer perspective: looking at work outside in, as a set of interconnected parts that connects the customer to what they want. In other words, considering an organisation as a customer would look at it and experiencing services as a customer would experience them. What that means is the path to fundamental improvement requires ignoring all internal functional boundaries. It also means ignoring external boundaries. It is the customer who is the arbiter of what constitutes the service boundaries and what is of value. A simple example is when a customer would like to take out a home loan. They may go to a mortgage broker who, in turn, liaises with a bank. From a customer's point of view, both the mortgage broker *and* the bank collectively provide the home loan service.

To examine a service organisation from a customer's perspective, it is critical to clearly define who the customer is. Some people think they have 'internal customers'. This is a confusing term and loses sight of the purpose of a service organisation. People within an organisation are not customers of each other – they are colleagues. Equally, third parties involved in providing a service, such as mortgage brokers described in the previous example, are sometimes considered to be customers. They are not. They might be important; however, they are part of the delivery of a service to a customer.

The tendency to overuse the term 'customer' has clouded its true meaning. We have found it useful to define the customer as follows:

> ☑ Customers are the people whom an organisation works together to serve, without which the service would not need to exist.

When leaders choose to look at their service organisation from a customer's perspective, they discover a unique source of improvement for creating a productive and positively viewed organisation that is better for customers, better for the organisation, and better for colleagues.

CLARITY OF PURPOSE

Once there is clarity about who is a customer, the next essential step is to clarify what the purpose of a service is from the customer's perspective, rather than the purpose developed from internal vision or mission statements.

It is important to describe the purpose as a customer would describe it. For example, if they were standing in front of you right now, what words would a customer use to define what the service does and why it exists from their perspective? In the case of adult social care, it could be to 'help me live the life I want to'. Clarity is essential, as is the need for the purpose to be described in concrete and measurable terms. Then it can be used to determine how productively the organisation services its customers and achieves the purpose the organisation has been set up to accomplish.

AN EXPERIENTIAL APPROACH

The above may sound like interesting theory. It is important to ask of any theory: *Could this work for me?*

When we work with leaders, we help them gain a customer's perspective of their organisation as a prelude to improvement. The starting point is for leaders to learn first-hand:

- The typical and predictable customer demands placed on their organisation, and how well their services are designed to deliver value for each of those demands

- The amount of unproductive activity (cost) inherent in the current organisational design and, more importantly, the causes of these costs

- How people experience their work, their leader, and the organisation

- How well organisational systems drive productive behaviour and activity

- The shared mythologies underpinning existing organisational culture

- What needs to be addressed to create productive organisational systems and structures to guide how work operates in the future

In our experience, through this experiential approach, leaders find that not one person in the organisation truly understands what creates value for their customers. The cost to both the organisation and the customer, by serving customers across different channels until the customer's wants and needs are met, is also not understood. Leaders see that failing to do something, or failing to do something right for a customer - known as failure demand (see chapter 11, Failure demand – The invisible expense) causes customers to place repeat demands on the organisation until they get what they need. They are surprised to learn that failure demand can account for as much as 80 per cent of all customer demand for their organisation. Equally, they are amazed to see the extent of unproductive activity, such as rework and duplication in their various end-to-end processes across channels. Leaders learn that their inability to easily respond to differing customer needs has led them to become exemplars in short-term repair, not long-term resolution. They quickly understand the economics: both failure demand and unproductive activities are hidden operational expenses, with no strategy or plan to remove them. Leaders see first-hand how policies, systems, processes, and rules designed into the organisation drive unproductive behaviour and activity, cause immense frustration, and hamstring their colleagues from effectively serving customers.

When people go through an experiential learning experience such as the above, dissonance is created. Dissonance is an experience where our expectations or predictions are challenged.

To put it simply, the data does not fit with the expectation. This is a challenge, major or minor, to our worldview. Dissonance can be positive or negative; it may come as a pleasant surprise or a nasty shock. Either way, something unpredicted has happened. Often, the experience of dissonance is profound. People experience a state of mind generated by the clear failure of a prediction that has been based upon a strongly held belief. They experience something they did not expect.

The experience of dissonance need not always be negative. The positive aspect of a shift of balance can be summed up in the phrase 'the penny dropped', or 'the light went on'. A clear example of this is encapsulated in the following reflections of an executive, recounting his experience of experiential learning:

> 66 *I thought Reconceive would come in and benchmark us against other organisations and confirm that we were best in the industry. We were proud of what we had done, the awards we had won, and the results we were getting.*
>
> *When I saw the opportunities for improvement for myself, it was confronting. It created a lot of dissonance.*
>
> *I saw first-hand what we had done to people's working life. We had done a really good job turning people into press button monkeys. We were controlling the process well, but there was no room for people to apply discretion and thought. I started thinking about it from their point of view. My reaction was, 'Oh no, what have I done?'*

These types of responses are not uncommon. It is like a mask being lifted from people's eyes. It also energises people, as they can see the massive scope for improvement which had previously been hidden. Once dissonance has been created, it is critical for each person to sense that any change will benefit them, the organisation, and customers, and that they are part of the change – it won't be rolled out, or 'done to them'.

Returning to the executive quoted above:

> 66 *I experienced a different way of looking at things in terms of value to customers and learned how you actually design your systems and structures to deliver on that value. The things I learned really resonated with me. I saw the need to completely rethink how you do things rather than tinker.*
>
> *As a result, we made a lot of improvement to the way people were working, and it was well received by customers and employees. There was relief from the front-line. There was also a lot of growth in the leadership team.*

Leaders assume experience is the same as knowledge. The assumption is that if leaders get together in a workshop or a meeting, brainstorm ideas for improvement, and then implement those ideas, better results will follow. Unfortunately, people are inhibited by their assumptions and underlying beliefs about work, organisation, and leadership. This prevents real opportunities to be seen. Seeing the organisation as a customer sees it shifts leaders' starting place from thinking they know what their problems are to discovering they have quite different problems to solve.

RECONCEIVING SERVICE DELIVERY REDUCES COSTS AND INCREASES CAPACITY

We believe in the principle that all customers deserve the same high-quality service. Working alongside people in the organisation, we use a process of experimentation that utilises new knowledge to inform improvements to be made. As a result, services are designed in a way to simultaneously provide exceptional service and, counterintuitively, reduce costs.

Once the service's purpose is delivered upon the first customer contact, failure demand and swathes of unproductive activity disappear and operational capacity increases. There are significant reductions in unwanted demand coming into the contact centre and other channels. Complaints and negative posts on social media are replaced by compliments and positive swings in advocacy. Customers switch to using digital services to search and fulfil rather than progress chase ('Where is my…?'). Churn falls dramatically, because when customers receive better value from their services, it engenders brand loyalty. Staff engagement scores improve as morale rockets. Improved financial results follow: operational expense falls and, in sales organisations, revenue increases.

To illustrate, a large Australian organisation was renowned for being difficult and painful to deal with. The organisation itself understood this and had established a specialist group to change and improve service. For several years, the organisation tried various change approaches, each of which failed to create any significant improvement. This was when we received a call. The leaders wanted to test our approach to determine whether it could be used to transform their fundamentally poor and negative customer experience reputation.

Once the predictable customer circumstances, needs, and issues were truly understood, the real nature of what customers wanted was indisputable. This knowledge enabled leaders to see important and counterintuitive phenomena for the first time, and revealed how conventional measures had kept this business-critical information hidden. They truly understood the problems created by the current organisational systems and structure and finally had a cohesive view of what needed to be challenged to improve. As a result, they agreed to see if a better service experience could be created to enable customers to more easily get value from their services. The outcomes of reconceiving and redesigning the service? After just a few months:

- The previous Net Promoter Score leapt by over a 100-point positive increase

- Failure demand generated by the organisation reduced from an astonishing 54 per cent to 5 per cent

- Staff absenteeism declined, from 12 per cent to 4 per cent

- Happier customers became loyal to the organisation and consequently purchased more products and services

Providing exceptional services by understanding what matters to customers, and enabling colleagues to work productively to service customers, will unlock similar profound improvements for you and your organisation.

11
FAILURE DEMAND – THE INVISIBLE EXPENSE

In the *Financial Times*, Sarah O'Connor warned: 'In the pursuit of efficiency, [call centres] have ground humanity out of their workers — the very quality they now want to get back … If the problem is that emotionally exhausted workers are giving a bad experience to customers, then a simpler solution would be to prevent them from getting so burnt out in the first place.'[44]

The results of this type of failed improvement approach for customers was accurately described by fellow columnist Camilla Cavendish in her article 'Press 1 for hell': '"Due to coronavirus, it will take longer to answer your call." Who, exactly, are they kidding? A year into the crisis, some of the biggest institutions

---

44 'It's creepy that AI is teaching workers to be more human', Sarah O'Connor, *Financial Times*, 14 Apr 2021.

are still blaming Covid-19 for their monstrous incompetence and callow indifference. All those hours saved on the commute by working from home are now being wasted in the vortex of banks, energy and phone companies' customer services whose idea of accountability is chatbots.'[45]

The service quality improvement and cost minimisation efforts described by O'Connor and Cavendish are indeed destined to fail. The reason for the futility of these approaches was identified over 30 years ago by John Seddon, the British occupational psychologist. He analysed the reasons why people contacted public and private sector organisations and found that routinely up to 80 per cent of the contacts made were avoidable. Seddon termed these unnecessary contacts 'failure demand'.

Failure demand is caused by failures to do something, or do something correctly, for the customer. It lurks everywhere a customer interacts with an organisation; for example, in the contact centre, retail store, field services, or digital channel. Because of failure demand, each channel frequently becomes a rework centre, patching up the results of faulty internal organisational systems and structures.

Organisations have unwittingly become very good at turning a customer demand into a failure demand. If that's not frustrating enough for customers, many organisations inadvertently **generate** failure demand. The following are two clear examples of how easy this is to achieve.

Case 1: A telecommunications organisation sent out letters to advise their customers that certain legacy services would be turned off. Many of the customers they mailed didn't even use those services, so these customers flooded the contact centre to ask, 'Does this apply to me?'

---

45 'Press 1 for hell: Covid is a flimsy excuse for dire customer service', Camilla Cavendish, *Financial Times*, 19 Mar 2021.

Case 2: A financial service organisation sent out computer-generated letters to their customers explaining there had been a change in the law and how it might affect their investments. The change only affected a small number of customers; however, it had been sent out to all customers 'just in case people were missed'. The organisation was flooded with enquiries from customers for whom the advice was irrelevant, which took them months to clear.

Both are clear cases of the organisations generating their own failure demand. Both are also clear examples of how service improvement programs are unaware of the hidden expense of failure demand.

Another example is when call centre contracts focus on cost per call, minimising call duration and fast pick-up times. But if, typically, 20 per cent, and as much as 80 per cent, of calls are unnecessary in the first place, handling them cheaper or faster makes marginal sense. Calls prompted by delivery problems, incorrect websites, confusing packaging, baffling instructions, incomprehensible forms, misunderstood advertising, or other internal organisational failures are simply repeat work. Empathy training programs are not the tool for this. The failures need to be stopped at their source.

Failure demand is such a simple concept, and understanding it and acting on it is one of the single greatest levers leaders have to improve digital and service delivery, increase capacity, and reduce operational expense. However, until leaders learn to see failure demand and, more importantly, permanently eliminate it once the root cause is identified and fixed, it remains an invisible problem.

REMOVING FAILURE DEMAND

Removing failure demand represents one of the greatest opportunities to improve service, increase capacity, and reduce operational expense in your business. Ignoring the nature of customer demand is to ignore one of the greatest levers you have to improve performance.

What is really required is the application of a different approach, where what creates value for customers and how best to service them sets the context for improvement, where people are organised and enabled to do that work more effectively, and where productive leadership practices are embedded. Then, technology needs to be quickly applied which complements the more effective operating model, which provides further value and further reduction in cost. This unique approach enables leaders to achieve the outcomes they are looking for in months, not years.

Why isn't everyone already doing this? Because it requires that the conventional assumptions and beliefs that shape behaviour about digital and service delivery, leadership, and culture be questioned and challenged.

To understand and challenge one's own assumptions, a leader needs to take a customer's perspective and spend time seeing for themselves what happens in their front-line (and back-office) operations. Senior executives are astonished when they realise the money wasted and damage inadvertently inflicted on their customers, employees, and brand. The good news is that they also quickly see the opportunity for improvement: stunning cost reductions and exceptional service delivery improvements are made visible.

An example of where this approach was adopted and the benefits realised is provided by Renato Mota, Chief Executive Officer of Insignia Financial. He recounts the experience at Insignia Financial when he and his leadership team understood and challenged their assumptions by taking a customer's perspective and spent time seeing for themselves what happened in the front-line:

66 *We went through a process of reframing. The process of reframing took us to a point that we realised going back is not an option. There reaches a point where you actually can't go back. Once your thinking changes, even a little bit, there's a point of no return.*

What does that look like? Taking very senior managers in the organisation into the call centre and listening to calls, understanding what is value.

A good example of understanding value: you'd be on a call, you'd be listening to one of the calls, the client calls in and says, 'I want to reset my password'. The call centre operator helps them reset their password and asks, 'Is there anything else you need to do?', the customer replies, 'No, that's all good, thanks', and hangs up.

We then go on to analyse that. Was that value? Did we create value? The first response is, 'Well, yeah, they wanted their password reset,' but I'm yet to meet someone who wakes up in the morning and wants their password reset. Fundamentally, they were trying to log on to do something – the reality is we didn't know what they were trying to do. We had no idea. That is just a small example. There were thousands of these examples every day.

The senior management team went through a process of resetting their minds around what value was and how much demand, both failure and value demand, was coming through our touchpoints. And we started with our call centre. I can tell you there was a tremendous amount of failure demand, either resetting passwords, following up transactions, following up communications we've sent to them that they didn't understand

— these were all sources of failure demand; demands that were being put on our system, at our expense, in a lot of times that we had created.

So, we learned we had a problem, a significant problem. Now, [it was] a problem in a relative sense; the business was performing well, but in the organisation, we were creating false demands, or failure demands, into our own organisation, and once you look at that through a different lens, you can't look at that and ignore it. We knew we had a problem.

How do you deal with the problem? Well, you've got to unpack those myths, unpack those assumptions. Whether we like to accept it or not, we are all full of assumptions, assumptions that SLAs and KPIs are going to lead to more efficient businesses. Assumptions around, well, surely if someone's on the phone for 10 minutes, rather than 2 minutes, that means the costs of running our business is going to be more expensive; this has got to be more expensive. There were a whole bunch of assumptions that we had to go through, reframing our own mindset. We couldn't say no to the opportunity once we had seen it with our own eyes.

The question remains: Are you ignoring one of the greatest levers you have for improving performance in your organisation?

12
THE KEY TO REDUCING COSTS AND PROVIDING EXCEPTIONAL SERVICE

What is exceptional customer service? This should be easy to answer; after all, there is a growing trend for people to talk about delivering 'exceptional customer experiences' and 'creating value for customers'. Well, unfortunately, this talk is just that, as there is no agreed definition for exceptional customer experience or customer value.

Language is important, and there should be clarity of definition behind these terms – they shouldn't be vague. To achieve clarity requires definitions to be anchored from the right perspective. In the case of service delivery, that perspective should be from a customer's point of view.

We have developed a specific, tangible definition that does just that:

☑️ Delivering exceptional customer experiences and creating value for customers requires meeting the customer's nominal value.

So, what does this mean and what does it look like? And how do we know it is being achieved? First, let's consider what is meant by nominal value.

The phrase nominal value was first coined by Genichi Taguchi, who was working in manufacturing in Japan in the 1950s. At the time, in manufacturing, it was common practice to make things to a specific standard, with some tolerance allowed. Provided that things were manufactured above the lower tolerance and below the upper tolerance, they passed inspection. Imagine a nut and a bolt: so long as the nut fits on the bolt, it passes. But standards with tolerances means there would still be some variation within that range in the final products delivered. In this example, the nut would fit, but not necessarily perfectly; there might be some variation and movement.

Taguchi asserted that manufacturing should abandon standards with tolerances and instead choose a nominal point on the continuum between upper and lower tolerances and call it the nominal value.

Taguchi then advised that production should strive to work towards that nominal value, manufacturing items closer and closer to the nominal value, thus reducing variation and getting closer to perfection. Taguchi postulated a theory of economic loss: the further any item is from the nominal value, the greater the loss (cost) to the overall system. In simple terms, more things go wrong, break down, or take longer to resolve. Taguchi described the optimal point for cost and value. It was a breakthrough. This is the secret behind world-class manufacturing: the continual reduction of variation equates to better quality, better consistency, and better performance.

In the late 1960s, Frank Pipp, an assembly plant manager for a Ford Motor Company factory, instructed his staff to purchase competitors' cars. His plan was to have the final assembly team disassemble these cars and learn first-hand how they [were] assembled.[46] When Pipp had his engineers take apart and reassemble a Toyota, they were speechless. Its parts just fit together, no banging was needed—they just "snap fit", like plastic Lego pieces.[47] This was Taguchi's nominal value and theory of economic loss in action.

THE NOMINAL VALUE IN SERVICE ORGANISATIONS

When manufacturing things, the **organisation** sets the nominal value. Standardisation in manufacturing is a good first step because the aim is to design out variation, to make things more and more alike because something physical is being made.

The practice of making things to a specific standard in manufacturing is, by definition, ignoring variation. However, when leaders try to apply this same logic to service organisations,

---

46 'Reflections on the fabric of the Toyota Production System', Bill Bellows, *Lean Management Journal* – Nov/Dec 2009, 7 Dec 2009.

47 Systemic Change Management: *The Five Capabilities for Improving Enterprises*, Anthony J. DiBella and George L. Roth, Palgrave Macmillan, 2015.

it just doesn't work. Service differs from manufacturing in several important respects:

- Nothing is 'stored' in the way products can be stored

- Service is not 'made' by physical (making things) means

- Service happens at the points of transaction

- Front-line employees are part of the service delivery

- The customer is involved in the service delivery

Let's use two simple examples to illustrate the differences. If you want to buy a tyre for your car, as a customer, you have limited choice on what tyre to buy. Thousands of tyres of the same type can be churned out by the same manufacturer with little variation. The only variables are which brand of tyre, based on what's available and what is suitable for your car. Tyres are a manufactured product that have been produced to a standard, so there is little variation in the product.

However, if you buy any goods online, then, as a customer, you might care about when the goods are delivered, what delivery options are provided, what methods of payment are available, what is the return policy, and so on. Customers are a key component in the 'production' of the service, and the resulting variation in customer demand can be vast. Hence, in service organisations, there is a need to adopt an approach that differs from manufacturing to deal with that variety of customer demand.

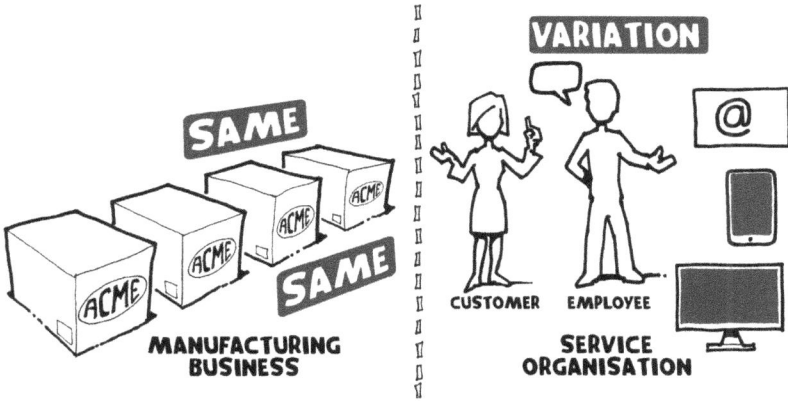

In service, it's the **customer** who sets the nominal value. Think of any service you encounter. If the service organisation understands your circumstances, needs, and issues, and responds to what matters to you (your nominal value), you have an exceptional customer experience and value is delivered.

If, for any reason, your service organisation does not recognise and respond to what matters to you, your experience of the service is unsatisfactory, and the service organisation consumes more resources to provide or rectify the service. If the experience is poor, it may also cause you to go to a competitor.

To give a simple example: you may ring a telco and ask for an internet connection to be installed. The agent informs you that you can have either an AM or a PM appointment. This is a standardised approach where the organisation has set the nominal value. As a customer, it's up to you to work out how to free up the whole morning or afternoon to wait at home for the technician to show up. If, on the other hand, the telco agent asked you what time worked for you, and the technician showed up exactly at that time, you would be amazed at the service. In this latter case, the service has been configured to deliver to meet **your** nominal value.

Using the example above, it may seem that the latter approach would be more expensive to deliver. However, counterintuitively, it is in instances such as the first case, when standardised services ignore the nominal value of customers, that the costs are **higher**. Unfortunately, it is the standardised service approach that dominates the service organisation, but just as Taguchi argued in manufacturing, the further a service organisation moves away from the customer's nominal value, the greater the loss/cost to the overall system. The Taguchi loss function predicts that if the service fails to meet the exact needs of any customer, it will incur losses. In practical terms, this means that if the service does not give customers what they want and in the way they want it (their nominal value), then the cost of service will rise. The traditional thinking is that having standardised services reduces costs. It is a flawed and costly assumption.

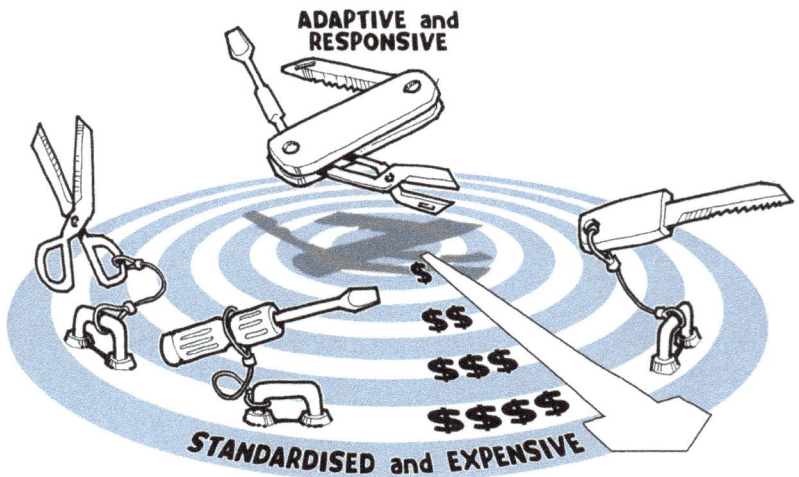

Think about how organisations seek to lower costs: they focus on lowering transaction costs by standardising services. The cost of transactions, however, tells leaders nothing about the cost of a service. What actually matters is the true cost of a service, not the transaction cost – in other words, the cost of delivering the total number of transactions it takes for customers to get a service.

Standardising service work drives costs up simply because a defining feature of many service organisations is the variety of customer demand that they must be able to absorb. If leaders push high-variety demand into standardised service, they will drive their costs up as the number of customers who do not fit the 'standard' service increases. The crucial factor is the complexity of the service.

The implementation of the UK Government's Universal Credit program illustrates very clearly the impact of servicing high-variety customer demand through the introduction of a standardised service.

Universal Credit was developed to replace a host of benefits, including council tax, job seeker's allowance, and housing benefits, into a single, standardised, digital-only system. On the face of it, the premise they adopted for implementing the program made sense – take costs out of a benefits service provision by putting the service provision online. However, the initial digital-access-only design has unravelled, as the reality of dealing with vulnerable people with multiple interrelated issues has dawned.

Multiple reports of hardship and operational failure continue to become fodder for tabloid stories.[48] An article in the *New Statesman*, a British political and cultural magazine, titled 'The Universal Credit nightmare shows there's nothing more dangerous than a good idea', stated: 'There's a cruel double bind here. Most people claim benefits precisely because they are in difficult personal circumstances. They have lost their job, got sick, or broken up with a partner and had to move house. Those same circumstances make dealing with bureaucracy more challenging. When the computer says no, it doesn't just take away one of half a dozen benefits; it can disrupt the only assistance people are getting. ... But this is

---

48   See, e.g., 'Universal credit has caused untold hardship. But the worst is yet to come', Frances Ryan, *The Guardian*, 31 Aug 2017.

the kind of detail that computer systems struggle to deal with: the hardest thing to build into any IT project is common sense.'[49] Universal Credit claimants epitomise high-variety customer demand. Unable to get what they want through the digital service, claimants ring the helpline because they want to speak to a human being to explain their context, that is, their circumstances, needs, and issues. The contact centres struggle to cope with 'unanticipated demand'. As a result, Universal Credit has had multiple announcements of delays. It was meant to be fully live by April 2017, but the most recent delay has pushed it to September 2024.[50] Implementation costs, initially forecast to be around £2 billion,[51] have racked up to over an eye-watering £16bn.[52] As this case study shows, providing a standardised service for high-variety customer demand can lead to dissatisfied customers and high financial impacts for the service organisation.

The question is, then, how does a service organisation deliver exceptional customer service and absorb high-variety customer demand without experiencing the same outcome as the Universal Credit program?

VARIETY VERSUS STANDARDISATION

Service creates value. Quality creates value. Both are concerned with the customer's emotional state and their expectations. What matters is how customers feel about an organisation. Whether the organisation is positively or negatively viewed will be determined by the way the service is designed and the interactions the customer has with the organisation.

---

49 'The Universal Credit nightmare shows there's nothing more dangerous than a good idea', Helen Lewis, *New Statesman*, Sep 2017.

50 'Universal credit rollout delayed again – to 2024', *BBC News*, 3 Feb 2020.

51 Universal credit, Wikipedia.

52 'Universal Credit costs leap by more than 20% to £15.8bn', *Computer Weekly*, Bryan Glick, 25 Jun 2015.

The assumption behind standardisation is that every customer is the same and wants the same. Typically, organisations will service customers in a standard way, designing a one-size-fits-all service. As a result, customers placing demands on the organisation are expected to fit in with what the service organisation offers and how they offer it. These demands go through various rules and processes that deliver outcomes. Leaders standardise that flow in an attempt to achieve efficiencies and economies of scale. This design is then cemented in technology.

Conventionally, leaders do not include in the design of a service the ability to absorb variety, because they believe that standardisation equals efficiency. Things like standardisation, which works well in manufacturing, creates massive failure demand in service systems as customers fight to get what *they* want from the service provider, rather than what the service provider's organisational systems design allows the customer to have. Leaders are generally oblivious to the costs their services carry that are due to the failure to give customers what they want. It is a hidden expense.

In service organisations, the needs of individuals vary dramatically, as do the outcomes they seek and the situations in which the service is delivered. Because people come with a variety of needs, leaders need to design services that can absorb that variety, with technology to support and enable it.

The problem leaders should be trying to solve is how to enable the front end of the service to understand and deliver what matters to customers, and at the rate and in the manner customers seek it. To give exceptional service to every customer at less cost, the task for leaders becomes one of configuring the organisation so that the customer sets the nominal value, not the organisation.

When it comes to creating digital services, the common assumption is that digital transactions are cheaper. However, as we pointed out earlier, this confuses transaction costs, which will be lower through a digital channel, with the true costs of service – in other words, the cost to deliver the total number of transactions it takes for customers to obtain a service.

When we work with leaders, we help them gain a customer's perspective of their organisation. They learn that they can't just digitise transactions and expect costs to reduce. The crucial factor is the complexity of each transaction. When what is being delivered is simple and unvarying, moving a transaction to digital channels may be effective. However, when the transaction is complex and variable, it is an expensive mistake which leaders see will inadvertently drive costs up and the quality of service down.

If you think about it, technology is simply a yes/no in terms of what it can do. Technology cannot deal with high-variety demand, and cannot understand human beings in their context, i.e., their circumstances, their needs, and their issues. Technology relies strictly on rules.

Well-intended leaders are mostly unaware of these pitfalls. Because large sums of money have been spent on a digital transformation, customers are pushed to use digital channels under the assumption that costs will reduce and a return on investment will be achieved. As a result, customers are coerced to transact through digital channels by channel switching (working to digital transaction targets, front-line employees instruct customers on how to use technology whenever they interact with the organisation), by financial penalties (customers are told it will cost more to transact with a person), by services being withdrawn (customers are told that certain transactions can now only be completed digitally), and by invitations to interact with a chatbot when visiting a website or download an app while waiting in a phone queue.

Instead of a digital-first or digital-only strategy, a better approach is to have a *customer-first* strategy. The approach to technology needs to be reframed. When what is delivered is simple and unvarying, moving transactions to digital channels may be more effective. However, when what is delivered is complex and variable, leaders should consider technology as something that should be designed to complement, not replace, human activity.

EXCEPTIONAL SERVICE COSTS LESS

Customers' views and judgements of service are formed from every transaction they have with an organisation. Unlike the traditional view of marketers, who think of the world as Brand → Reputation → Transaction, a customer's perception of value is, in fact, reversed: Transaction → Reputation → Brand. Desirability means focusing on improving every transaction the customer has with the organisation in terms of what matters to that customer, and in doing so, reputation is built, as is the brand. The organisation then becomes positively viewed.

There is no balance between service and cost. Although counterintuitive, it is possible to improve customer satisfaction *and* save money at the same time. To achieve this, it is critical for leaders to focus their attention on managing value, not costs. This means stripping away assumptions about standardisation and costs and asking how the organisation can configure itself to understand and deliver what matters to customers.

The starting point is to learn what creates value for customers by understanding their circumstances, needs, and issues. The next step is to service customers by the most effective means, wherever they interact with the organisation: getting it right for the customer the first time by designing services that are adaptable and responsive, not standardised. (See Systems that equalise and differentiate, page 139, in chapter 14.)

If organisations truly understand what matters to their customers and design services to meet the customers' nominal value, supported by technology, customers receive an exceptional experience and value is always delivered. You no longer have to face tough choices between reducing costs and improving service. Instead, you sustainably improve customer satisfaction and increase capacity, while reducing costs. The result is a win for the customer and for the service organisation.

An example of where this approach was adopted and the benefits realised is provided by Danik Lucas, an executive at WorkCover Queensland. He recounts the results achieved at WorkCover Queensland when he and his leadership team designed services to meet the customers' nominal value:

> 66 *After studying our systems, we were shocked to learn that 82% of demand was failure demand.*
>
> *We learned that what mattered to our customers was a quick decision on their claim. We can now measure that directly in customer terms.*
>
> *The more we eradicated failure from the system, the more it released capacity. That extra capacity has enabled us to make quicker and more claim decisions. We are now able to determine claims over 70% faster, with over 40% of claims determined the same or next day.*
>
> *The result: even though our front-line may need longer for up-front work, they've now got additional capacity during each day. Because they get it right up-front, they don't have to spend unproductive time dealing with failure demand during the day. It is more than net neutral; there is additional capacity, hence we're able to make more claim decisions per day with the same number of people.*
>
> *By doing this, there is no doubt that we've delivered an improvement for customers. The feedback we've had is that our customers are amazed by the improved service.*

13
WHAT DRIVES UNPRODUCTIVE BEHAVIOUR AND ACTIVITY?

For society or an organisation to prosper, there must be social cohesion, agreed arrangements about what is acceptable and/or productive behaviour and activity. However, not all people behave in constructive or productive ways. Why might that be the case?

Often, we see people behaving in ways that we do not understand. A simple and rather lazy way to explain, or perhaps dismiss, that behaviour is to categorise it as mad, bad, and/or stupid.

What follows is a smorgasbord of short examples of unproductive behaviour and activity. Remember, as you read these: they are **real-life** examples. Some may even sound eerily familiar.

Following on from the examples, we aim to provide a deeper understanding of what might be causing or driving those behaviours, rather than the simplistic classification of the behaviour and activity as mad, bad, and/or stupid.

EXAMPLES OF UNPRODUCTIVE BEHAVIOUR AND ACTIVITY

Case 1: In a financial services organisation, customers were sent letters to inform them that they had been pre-approved for $10,000 personal loans. All the customer had to do was call the contact centre, or go online, and confirm that they wanted the loan. Customers started calling the contact centre asking for something other than $10,000 loan amounts, for example, $8,000 or $12,000, as the online forms had no option to specify the amount. The contact centre salespeople told each customer who didn't want exactly $10,000 that they couldn't have the amount requested – the disgruntled customers replied they would go elsewhere. Why did the salespeople knowingly give up sales? Because only loans of exactly $10,000 resulted in them receiving a bonus.

Case 2: In another organisation, employees were aware that technology had been installed that tracked what applications they used on their computer during office hours. Some people in the IT department wrote a program that made the mouse hover over the work administration application, regardless of the actual application in use. The program constantly gave a little wobble of the mouse pointer over the work administration application, thus fooling the tracking software into gauging that work was being done on that application. The workers appeared to be 100 per cent utilised. Managers were extremely happy, but they were in the dark as to what was really going on.

Case 3: Mystery shoppers were engaged by a retail organisation to ensure customers were receiving a great experience whenever they shopped at their stores. The idea was that the mystery shopper would rate the store employees on things like how friendly and approachable they were, their product knowledge, how long they had taken to do things, if they had made the sale, and if they had attempted to upsell additional products to the customer. The mystery shopper would note down performance and write the results in a report for head office. The store manager would then receive a rating for their store. To incentivise the store employees to do their best, the organisation decided that a percentage of their monthly pay would be based on the mystery shopper performance rating. The store employees worried about losing pay. However, they soon began to recognise the mystery shoppers through tell-tale signs; for example, the mystery shopper would take notes, check their watch, would be on their own, and talk to multiple store employees before purchasing. This led the store employees to over-service the mystery shopper and ignore real customers who were in the store. The mystery shopper numbers looked good, but sales declined and complaints increased.

Case 4: In a sales organisation, when salespeople had reached their targets for the month, they were unhappy when additional customers contacted them that month wanting to purchase products. The reason for their unhappiness was because if they exceeded their monthly sales targets, then the following month's target would be increased. To work around this issue, the salespeople would file new sales away until the beginning of the following month, and process them at that time. This led to an increase in unhappy customers chasing the progress of their purchases, and often lost sales.

Case 5: In another organisation, internal users were asked to perform user acceptance testing (UAT) on newly built technology. They were pressured to meet an arbitrary one-week testing deadline. Despite finding multiple issues with the new technology, once the UAT time was up, the users doing the testing were told that they could either sign off that the technology was acceptable, or go without the new technology completely, and wait until the next scheduled release the following quarter. The users were left with little choice but to accept and sign off on the knowingly flawed technology. Despite the activity being called user acceptance testing, it had everything except the acceptance bit; the users tested the software, but there was no acceptance, just resignation. The technology was installed and, post-release, the only thing the users could do was log each bug with the help desk in the hope that the bugs would be fixed in the future.

Case 6: Managers of one business unit would engage in all kinds of behaviour designed to make their numbers look right. For example, they would delay critical work until the new financial year began, agree with suppliers to bill in the next financial year for work completed in the current year, and claim 'unexpected budget balances' that necessitated carrying forward those balances into the new financial year. What shouldn't be normal had become the norm.

Case 7: An organisation had spent millions on their new digital services. It was trumpeted as a success. The senior managers called the new services wonderful, and praised things like the removal of paper-based work, elimination of convoluted processes, and the cost reduction that resulted when several full-time employees were supplanted by the technology. They would demonstrate the new technology in internal marketing videos using their tablets or smartphones. As each new digital service was released, the thinking was that the old service and the new would run in parallel, until everything a customer did in the old service was replicated in the new digital service, at which point the old service could be decommissioned. The problem was that as each new service was brought online, customers kept going back to the old, rather than using the new. This was because the customers either didn't like the new digital service or it didn't do what they needed it to do. Irritated, management decided to turn off the old services to force customers to use the new digital services. Apart from the customers, who was the hardest hit by this decision? The complaints management team.

Case 8: A CX team had completed some research on what annoyed customers when they interacted with the organisation's contact centre. One of the most common complaints was being transferred between agents or departments. As a result of this research, the CX team launched an internal campaign called 'Targeting transfers'. The idea was that an agent could only transfer a maximum of five customers per day. The agents were expected to use their initiative to solve a customer's problem, rather than simply transferring them. Initiative was used, just not in a productive way. The numbers looked good, as very few agents exceeded the five customers transfer limit. How was this achieved? When the agent hit their transfer limit, if a customer they talked to later that day needed to be transferred, they would either disconnect the customer or tell the customer there was a 'problem with their computer' and give the customer the phone number of the correct department to call, and ask them to call back.

Case 9: In a large retailer, customers were asked to rate their experience as they left a store. At each exit there were happy, neutral, and sad face buttons to press. Every face button pressed was immediately recorded and appeared in a database in head office to form part of a weekly report. A ladder of the best and worst stores was produced. Arguments ensued for those who were the worst, leading to coercion of staff to do better. What do you suppose the staff did all day when there were quiet times, and no one was looking? Hammer the happy face buttons, of course.

RATING

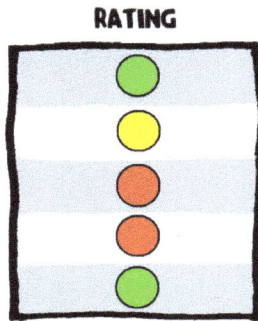

Case 10: In a contact centre, agents were rated by customers at the end of each call. The idea was that customers could give the agent a rating between 1 (very poor) to 10 (amazing service). The thinking was that ratings would give customers an opportunity to provide immediate feedback on how well (or not) the organisation had performed, and agents would receive coaching from their team leaders based on their scores. The problem was that agents were at the mercy of the types of calls they would receive. If the call was from a customer wanting to buy something, then usually the score was good. However, if the call was from a customer due to the organisation having failed to do something, or do something right for them (failure demand), they would typically receive a low score. The majority of the calls

coming into the contact centre were failure demand. To get around the system, agents would play 'telephone chicken': if the customer was unhappy at the end of a call, the agent wouldn't put the phone down, which meant the customer wasn't able to rate their call. This meant that phone calls would sometimes last for hours with neither the agent nor the customer giving up and putting the phone down.

Case 11: In another contact centre, the agent who took the most phone calls for the month received an extra day's holiday in recognition. The numbers of calls per agent were displayed on a screen on the wall. Some agents, who wanted the extra holiday, discovered that if they gave the customer their direct number and then put the phone down midway through the call, the customer would have to call back, thus one call became two. If the customer had two queries on the same call, they were informed by the agent to call back once the first query was complete. Thus, the number of calls per agent shot up; however, so did customer frustration.

Case 12: A repair organisation's answer to reducing costs was to ask technologists to build automated robots that could listen and respond to customer fault repair requests via artificial intelligence. A human-sounding voice would greet the customer, listen to what they had to say, run through a series of algorithms, and respond. When a customer rang in, the first three options in the menu led them to a robot. The fourth option took the customer to a human being. The leaders wanted to encourage the customers to use the new robots. Therefore, they didn't want people pressing option four (it was deemed more expensive to talk to a human). Using their ingenuity, the technologists programmed in a long delay between options three and four. The thinking was that a customer, upon hearing a pause after option three, would think there must only be three options to choose from and choose one of the first three options, which, in turn, would be cheaper for the organisation. If, after pressing either option one, two or three, a customer hung up midway through talking to a robotic voice, an automated fault report was generated, and an engineer was dispatched to the customer's house via a digitised workflow. When the engineer arrived at the customer's house only to find there wasn't a problem (logged as 'no fault found' on their iPad), the customer was sent a bill for the engineer's visit. It is easy to imagine the resulting complaints and failure demand coming from those customers.

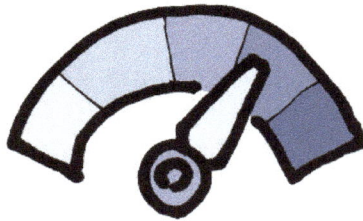

Case 13: In another organisation, sales staff would receive prizes for sales made, for example, they could win appliances like fridges, freezers, TVs, games consoles, and so on, if they hit their weekly targets. Sales did indeed go up, however, so did the number of returns. Sales staff were adding more units to an order to achieve their target (and win their prize). For example, one customer ordered five units but received 10 instead. Perplexed, the customer rang the supplier and was told it must have been a mistake and was asked to return the additional five units. It hadn't been a mistake. The salesperson had doubled the order number to win their prize. It was a regular practice.

Case 14: In the UK, hospitals have targets to meet. The official target requires 95% of patients to be treated, assessed or discharged within four hours, a figure the NHS has failed to meet since July 2015.[53] NHS managers are accused of leaving patients in vehicles so they can meet the target to treat everyone within four hours of being admitted to accident and emergency.[54] Meanwhile, an A&E consultant from the south of England said there were various ways to manipulate the statistics, including moving patients around the computer system to give the impression they had been relocated to elsewhere in the hospital.[55]

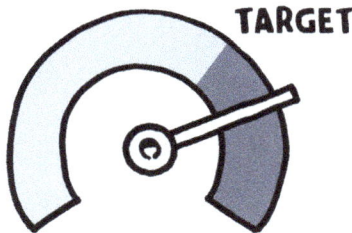

Case 15: Victorian police were given a target of 3 million breath tests for 2019–2020. In order to hit the target of 99.5 per cent of negative roadside breath tests, an internal police investigation found that more than 258,000 breath tests were estimated to have been falsified by Victoria Police officers to return negative readings. Officers had been found to either place a finger over the straw of the entry hole of the breath testing equipment

53 'A&E stats may have to be recalculated', Dr Faye Kirkland, *BBC News*, 22 Jan 2018.

54 'Don't leave patients in ambulances to hit A&E targets, hospitals told', Robert Watts and Laura Donnelly, *The Telegraph*, 27 Oct 2012.

55 'Doctors 'being pressurised into manipulating patient records to meet A&E targets', Shehab Khan, *The Independent*, 27 Jan 2018.

or blowing into the straws themselves.[56] This negative impact of targets on policing extends further – in the UK, police were set a target to achieve more convictions for violent crime. To reach the target, police officers who attended incidents like children fighting in a playground would book the children for violence.[57]

Case 16: In the Australian Banking Royal Commission final report, Commissioner Kenneth Hayne lamented, "'Providing a service to customers was relegated to second place. Sales became all important.'" He went on to say, "'Rewarding misconduct is wrong. Yet incentive, bonus and commission schemes throughout the financial services industry have measured sales and profit, but not compliance with the law and proper standards.'"[58] The culture of competition uncovered in the Royal Commission meant that, by definition, someone must lose, and often that loser turned out to be the customer. Recent findings from research by the Finance Sector Union concluded that two years after the Royal Commission handed down its findings, the banking culture was 'worse than ever'.[59] They found Australia's banks responded to the Royal Commission by implementing a process of changing and renaming targets, rather than addressing the underlying design of performance management systems. Consequently, the culture inside the banks has not improved. People still work within a toxic sales culture, with leaderboards and targets. The purpose of the front-line work remains the same: 'Hit the target'.

---

56   'Victoria Police could still be conducting false breath tests, anti-corruption watchdog warns', Bridget Rollason, *ABC News*, 30 Oct 2019.

57   'Deliverology', Beyond Command and Control, Vanguard Consulting.

58   Banking royal commission report takes axe to sales culture in finance, Michael Janda, *ABC News*, 4 Feb 2019.

59   '"Worse than ever": Australian bank culture has not improved since royal commission, staff say,' Ben Butler, *The Guardian*, 7 Apr 2021.

Case 17: An award-winning financial services organisation decided to improve their reputation by building an app where customers could see their account details on their smartphones without having to log in online or call the contact centre. The task was outsourced by the marketing department to an external agency who built it at considerable expense. The completed app looked fantastic on all devices and was extremely responsive. However, no one from the external agency had talked to the organisation's IT department about how the app would interface with the organisation's other IT systems, a seemingly obvious step in the development process, but not undertaken due to an unresolved standoff between the Head of Marketing (who wanted the work outsourced) and Head of IT (who wanted the work completed inhouse). Once the app was built, it was tested by internal technologists. It certainly had a slick-looking interface, but, unsurprisingly, the app had trouble talking to the organisation's internal IT systems. Ignoring this clear shortcoming, the organisation launched the app. Customers duly installed the app and shortly thereafter vented their frustration on the app review pages and on social media at how useless it was. The contact centre team bore the brunt of customer frustration. In the customer 'Ratings and Review' section for the app, the overall rating by customers ended up

being 1 star out of a possible 5. However, rather than respond to this poor rating, the leaders were largely unperturbed. In fact, they admitted that the only reason they had asked for an app to be created was to achieve a 5-star rating award. The award givers had a tick box that said, 'You must have an app', not 'You must have an app that is useful for customers'. A 5-star rating for the organisation was considered far more important than a 5-star rating from customers.

Case 18: In a software design organisation, a monthly dashboard had showed a decreasing level of bugs found. Concerned about quality, technologists had been offered an incentive to find more bugs. Ever keen to receive the incentive, technologists programmed bugs into the software and then 'found' them![60]

The unproductive behaviour and activity described in each of the example cases above might have concerned and disturbed. Sadly, these examples are not unique. We have not cherry-picked the most shocking. We see the same, or similar, in all organisations that we have worked in around the world, be they private sector, public sector, or voluntary organisations.

---

60 'Incentives cause distortion', Beyond Command and Control, Vanguard Consulting.

SYSTEMS DRIVE BEHAVIOUR

We acknowledge that it would be easy to categorise all of the unproductive behaviour and activity described in these cases as mad, bad, and/or stupid, which begs the question: Why are we so quick to blame other people? The short answer is because it is easy. What this book aims to do is provide a deeper understanding of what might be causing or driving this unproductive behaviour and activity, rather than the simplistic conclusion that the people are to blame.

Any good organisational theory uses defined terms and specifies the relationships between and among them. The first term we need to define here is what is productive behaviour and activity. There are many differing views of what this constitutes but we have found it useful to define productive behaviour and activity as follows:

Behaviour and activity that achieves the purpose the organisation has been set up to accomplish.

We also need to understand what drives behaviour, be it productive or unproductive. Karl Stewart coined the phrase 'systems drive behaviour' when he was developing a theoretical understanding of systems.[61] We also contend that, as one of the fundamental tools of leadership, systems drive behaviour, a conclusion that has been reinforced by our observations over 25 years of working in service organisations.

---

61 Ian Macdonald, Catherine Burke and Karl Stewart, *Systems Leadership: Creating Positive Organisations*, 2nd edition, Routledge, 2018.

So, what are systems and why are they so important? Again, having a clear definition is the starting point. In this case an organisational system is defined as:

☑️ A framework that orders and sequences activity within an organisation to achieve a purpose.

The importance of systems stems from the fact that they operate all the time, all day, every day. Unlike leadership behaviour, systems are ever present, and they don't get tired or dispirited. As each of the cases above have shown, systems drive perfectly normal human beings to act in abnormal ways. Because systems drive behaviour, it is critical that leaders understand the relationship between the system design, their own behaviour, and the behaviour being driven in others. It is the work of leadership to understand this relationship and how productive it is.

Put in simple terms, leadership behaviour is what a leader does and says, whereas systems are the way things are done. To avoid confusion, leadership behaviour and systems design must not contradict each other. For example, suppose a leader behaves as if individual targets are unproductive, but uses targets in an appraisal to rate individual performance. In this case, people will at best be confused, or at worst, cynical.

There are a plethora of leadership books and courses to advise a leader how they should behave in order to improve the organisation: be charismatic and inspiring, more human, good at setting direction, be a good communicator, and be a good listener.

However, running a successful organisation over time cannot be done by leadership behaviour alone. There must be structures and systems that can survive individuals.

We have seen many leaders burn out when trying to influence systems by their leadership behaviour alone. For example, one leader thought that their job was to whisper in everybody's ear in an attempt to influence a change in behaviour. Unfortunately, they worked in an organisation of over two thousand employees – those are a lot of ears to whisper into. Despite the whispering, behaviour didn't change, as the organisational systems remained unchanged.

CREATING A PRODUCTIVE ORGANISATION

Leaders ask people to do their best, but most often, they already are. It was Deming who stated, 'A bad system will beat a good person every time'.[62] This view of systems supports our notion that every person we meet in a service organisation is always well-intended and highly motivated to deliver their best possible work. But in our experience, their best efforts are undermined by the way organisational systems and structures are designed and organised.

Leadership is about enabling people to act in a way that results in productive social cohesion. The holy grail for leaders is to influence others to behave constructively, productively, and creatively, so that people come to a place of work and willingly contribute to the purpose the organisation has been set up to accomplish.

Leaders try their best to improve their organisations using whatever tools they have available. For example, they may have been advised that people require motivation to improve performance. Following this advice, leaders put in place extrinsic 'motivators', such as leaderboards, incentives, targets, and service level agreements, but are left confused and disappointed when expected improvements do not follow.

---

62 The W. Edwards Deming Institute, February 1993, Deming Four-Day Seminar, Phoenix, Arizona (via the notes of Mike Stoecklein).

In our experience, to build a productive organisation where people willingly give their best requires the use of coherent theory, practical methods, leadership tools, and consistent and persistent leadership.

The following chapters articulate the benefit of a more coherent, systematic, and proven approach to enable progressive leaders to create an environment of clarity where people willingly come to work and positively contribute to delivering the purpose the organisation has been set up to accomplish.

14
LIBERATING PEOPLE AND ORGANISATIONS FROM STULTIFYING SYSTEMS

Every person we meet in a service organisation is invariably well-intended and highly motivated to deliver their best possible work. But, in our experience, their best efforts can be undermined by the way organisational systems have been designed and implemented. In short, the activities performed, and the way people behave at work are influenced more by organisational systems than the choices made by individuals.

This might seem counterintuitive. Surely, individual performance is tied to things like work efficiency, skill, quality of work, ability to learn, experience, motivation, engagement, meeting objectives, having an open mindset, and so on, yes?

And, surely, people who are high performers, team players, or even bad hires prove that what we contend is untrue, yes?

While these are reasonable questions, the influence organisational systems have on individual performance cannot be overestimated. Let's consider a typical service and maintenance organisation, and imagine for a moment that you work as one of their service and repair technicians. In this scenario, your organisation provides servicing, repair, and maintenance services for home appliances. The structure you work within and interact with comprises a branch manager, contact centre, scheduling team, and logistics department.

Customers contact the organisation to report that their appliances aren't working or need servicing. The contact centre consultants are trained in rudimentary diagnostic skills and do their best to ascertain the fix required. Each resulting job order is input into a workflow tool and is passed from the contact centre consultant to the scheduling team, who, based on targets of jobs per person per day, allocates you, as the service and repair technician, to a set of jobs for the next day.

A colleague in the logistics department organises the parts from the warehouse and ensures they are available for you to load in your van each morning. The next morning, you load your van and turn up at the various jobs at the scheduled times. For each job that day, the diagnosis was done correctly by the contact centre, you have all the parts you need to repair and service the appliances, and you have the skills and knowledge to do so. When you return to your branch at the end of the day, your manager congratulates you on your performance – you turned up at each job on time, all your jobs were completed within the specified times, and no complaints were received from customers.

The next day, the same process is followed, except this time when you turn up on time at a customer's premises, the appliance issue has been misdiagnosed by the contact centre consultant. You, therefore, have the wrong parts in your van, and you must tell the customer that you cannot fix their appliance. You follow procedure and advise the customer that they must ring the contact centre to tell them they need to book another appointment, and you fill in a form on your iPad to tell logistics what spare is needed. You attend two more misdiagnosed jobs that day. When you return to your branch, this time your manager isn't as happy as he was the day before. He tells you that you need to do better the next day, your productivity is 'lacking', and he's received some complaints from customers.

What accounts for the difference in performance? Not you as the technician, and not your skills, knowledge, or experience. It is the organisational systems that you are working within.

As one of the fundamental tools of leadership, we contend that systems drive behaviour – a conclusion that has been reinforced by our observations over 25 years of working in service organisations.

There are excessive levels of unproductive activity and wasted effort driven by poorly designed organisational systems in most organisations. In addition to the service and maintenance example, you will have read many other examples in this book, including 'chapter 5, It Just Works – A customer's dream?' and 'chapter 13, What drives unproductive behaviour and activity?' In this chapter, we demonstrate how to liberate people and organisations from stultifying systems to enable productive behaviour and activity, thereby creating a more positively viewed and productive organisation.

ORGANISATIONAL SYSTEMS AND BEHAVIOUR

Organisational systems are defined as:

☑️ A framework that orders and sequences activity within an organisation to achieve a purpose.

Designing productive systems is a major leverage point for improvement in organisational performance. Productive systems provide the framework to help an organisation turn their purpose into a positive and productive day-to-day experience for both customers and employees. The following real-life case study demonstrates how.

This particular organisation is one that delivers services to a wide range of customers. Customers place high levels of demand, of varying complexity, on the organisation. Some demands are transactional in nature and could be dealt with by the front-line. Other demands require managing over a longer term by other teams. To add to the complexity, various stakeholders are involved in helping the organisation deliver services to its customers.

The executive leadership identified the need to improve customer service, become more efficient, reduce operational expense, and increase employee engagement. They had, though, become frustrated by the inability of traditional change approaches, fads, and magic cures to achieve these improvements.

We worked with the leadership to help them gain a customer's perspective of the organisation as a prelude to improvement. Through an experiential exercise, they learned first-hand:

- The typical and predictable customer demands placed on their organisation, and how well their services were designed to deliver value for each of those demands

- The amount of unproductive activity (cost) inherent in the current organisational design and, more importantly, the causes of these costs

- The impact the organisational systems had on productive behaviour and activity

The leadership learned that their current organisational systems were causing high levels of failure demand, lots of unproductive activity, increased backlogs of work, and unneeded operational expense. Despite high customer satisfaction survey scores, they were shocked to learn that many customers had a negative view of the organisation.

These results disturbed the leadership. They were proud of the high-quality workforce employed in the organisation. They had set a high bar with their hiring criteria. Candidates were assessed on their technical skills, interpersonal skills, experience, self-motivation, culture fit, and more. The criteria had been set even higher for internal and external recruitment for managerial positions. There had been investment in training courses to develop people. Speakers had been invited to lunch sessions to inspire people and teach them new things. A staff suggestion portal had been set up. Offices had been redesigned to be more modern, open, and collaborative. The leaders had assumed that all these changes would translate into better performance. As these changes signify, their focus had been on the individual, but they had completely ignored the role and importance of organisational systems.

The next perspective of the organisation that we helped the leadership gain was the one held by their employees. The leaders went through another experiential learning process, understanding:

- How people experienced their work, their leader, and the organisation

- Shared mythologies underpinning the existing organisational culture

Whenever we work with leaders during these experiential learning exercises, we ask them not to intervene with the work being done. The purpose is for them to observe, learn, and reflect. If they attempt to intervene, it might help fix something they see at that point in time; however, as soon as they turn their back, the system reverts. As we say to leaders, their organisational systems are perfectly designed to produce the results they are getting and the issues they are seeing. Intervening at the personal level isn't going to systemically solve issues or improve results.

Rather than intervening and attempting to fix, we advise that it is better to ask questions. This reveals the true problems to solve.

When observing the work, some of the leadership asked colleagues if they could just ignore some of the red tape or not perform certain activities that obviously, to them, added no value. Their colleagues' response was always the same: they couldn't, because the policies, systems, processes, rules, or the IT didn't allow for such judgement or discretion. The leadership quickly learned that no team members, team leaders, or even senior managers had the authority to change an organisational system.

The leaders asked people what their managers paid attention to. They learned that managers were predominantly managing using the following equation: 'How much work have we got?' plus 'How long does it take to do the work?' plus 'How many people do I need to do the work?' These three questions drove managerial decision-making. Managers were fixated on managing people's activity – how many things they did, how long it took them to do each task, what was in their queue, and so on. This had created a burgeoning and bureaucratic measurement system. Employees were regularly monitored and surveilled using technology to feed the measurement system.

When people were asked what their managers do to improve productivity, typical responses revolved around trying to get people to do more work, work faster, automating work, standardising work, setting targets and service levels, creating procedures, scheduling, prioritising work, and hiring more people. Not one manager focused on improving organisational systems.

The morale of people who worked in the organisation had appeared reasonably good on the surface, with high engagement scores from annual employee engagement surveys, and middle management's view that 'everything was awesome'. Based on this information, the leadership quite reasonably predicted that the employee view of the organisation would be positive. However, after speaking to a cross-section of employees, they quickly learned that there was a high degree of dissatisfaction below the surface and that, overall, the organisation was negatively viewed by its employees.

The experiential learning process from both the customer and employee perspectives had diagnosed significant and previously hidden improvement opportunities in how to better service customers, work more efficiently, reduce operating costs, and improve engagement. The leaders now understood the relationship between systems design, their own behaviour, and the behaviour being driven in others. They still had a high-quality workforce that they could be proud of – that wasn't the problem. Instead, the leadership could now see that work undertaken by their high-quality workforce had been made harder over time due to the poor design and integration of organisational systems.

THE IMPORTANCE OF SYSTEMS

Designing and implementing productive systems is one of the biggest leverage points a leader has to create a more positively viewed and productive organisation. The fact that the managers in this organisation had given little attention to systems design and implementation is not uncommon. It is the same in almost every organisation with which we have worked. The lack of focus on systems is due to three reasons:

- the significance of systems is either unknown or misunderstood, as in the case study above

- the complexity of system design work is underestimated and/or delegated too low in the organisation

- leaders have no coherent theory to guide the design of productive systems

Once the importance of systems was understood, the next step was helping the leaders analyse their own organisational systems. To do so, it was important for them to be able to distinguish between the different types of systems in their organisation. The first distinction was to understand the difference between systems of equalisation and systems of differentiation, and which system was appropriate in a given situation.

SYSTEMS THAT EQUALISE AND DIFFERENTIATE

Systems that equalise treat all employees within an organisation the same, regardless of role or context. For example, a health and safety system applies to all layers within an organisation – no one, not even the CEO, is exempt from acting in a safe manner and being held to account for their behaviour. Systems that equalise can also apply to an organisation's customers; for example, data for all customers should be kept safe and secure.

Systems that differentiate treat people differently depending on their context. The basic principle of systems that differentiate is that all differences should be based on the work being done. An example of this is a remuneration system – a CEO works at a different level of capability to people who work at the front-line, with each being paid an amount that reflects the different level of complexity in their work. Similarly, systems that differentiate are present in customer interactions. For example, the different circumstances, needs, and issues for each customer demand placed on an organisation can be vast; a system of differentiation should ensure that this variety can be absorbed by designing services that are adaptable and responsive. (See chapter 12, The key to reducing costs and providing exceptional service.)

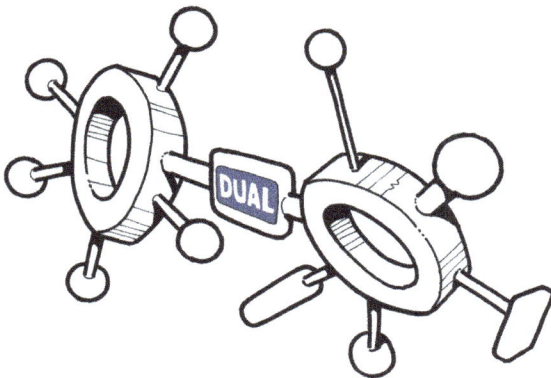

STANDARDISED

EQUALISING and DIFFERENTIATING

To create a positively viewed and productive organisation, there is a need for a mix of systems that equalise and/or differentiate. Most systems are designed based on the common misconception that it is better for systems to treat everything the same; in other words, equalise or standardise.

When analysing their own organisational systems, the leaders found that this misconception manifested in many significant ways. Examples included requiring all back-office employees to complete the same volume of work per day, ignoring the different levels of work complexity and individual capability, resulting in work being skipped or tasks being missed; and all customers being exposed to the same service level regardless of their context, resulting in customers initially receiving a standard automated 'We are working on it' message within 48 hours, which ignored individual customer circumstances, needs, and issues.

Management had fallen into a common trap of thinking that good system design is about making things equal and standardised. It is a common assumption that if everything is equalised, costs will reduce and productivity will increase. When examining the unintended impacts of their standardised system designs, the leaders learned that the opposite was true. Making things equal and standardised ignored the reality that systems involving humans need to be designed in a way that accommodates the complexity that humans bring. They learned that to create a more positively viewed and productive organisation, their systems need to be a mix of ones that equalised and/or differentiated based on context, rather than a one-size-fits-all approach.

AUTHORISED AND PRODUCTIVE SYSTEMS

There is an additional and equally important dimension to assessing the effectiveness of organisational systems, and that is whether the systems are authorised/unauthorised and productive/unproductive.

In simple terms, the purpose of any system is to produce a productive outcome for customers and employees. This is best achieved when a system is well designed and implemented, is authorised (approved by the organisation), and drives productive behaviour and activity (contributes to achieving the purpose of the organisation). Therefore, to create a positively viewed and productive organisation, the challenge is to ensure that every system is authorised and productive.

The leadership used a systems matrix to diagnose each of their organisational systems to determine whether it was authorised or unauthorised, and productive or unproductive. (See Table 1, Systems Matrix, below.)

	PRODUCTIVE	UNPRODUCTIVE
AUTHORISED	A Well designed and implemented	B Restrictive processes or practices that have emerged over time
UNAUTHORISED	C People 'cutting corners' to get things done	D Alternative leadership based on power

Table 1: Systems Matrix

The leadership was shocked to find that not one of their systems was well designed and implemented (box A). Many systems were best described as authorised and unproductive systems (box B). For example, the leaders diagnosed that their customer service system design resulted in high levels of failure demand and unproductive activity due to restrictive red tape (detailed policies, processes, rules, and restrictive technology) that had increased over time and had, in turn, led to high levels of customer and employee dissatisfaction. The intention had always been to design productive and authorised systems (box A). However, leaders had been let down by a lack of coherent theory and practical methods, and their systems had drifted into unproductive systems (box B) due to restrictive or misguided systems design.

When systems are authorised and unproductive, people may cut corners and use workarounds to deliver innovation and improvement. This leads to the creation of unauthorised but nevertheless productive systems (box C). Some of these systems did exist in the organisation. Unfortunately, though, leaders found these systems were often quickly quashed, and people admonished due to a lack of perceived compliance. In fact, middle management had doubled down in the creation of more rigid risk and compliance systems to stop future workarounds and corner-cutting. Stymieing efforts to improve systems had resulted in them drifting slowly into becoming unauthorised and unproductive (box D), a system that sets up an alternate leadership based on power. A clear case of this was where middle managers would bypass team leaders and directly assign work to team members to try to increase output. Despite using power by overstepping agreed lines of authority, middle managers would still hold team leaders to account for not hitting productivity targets.

Although a sobering and salutary experience, being able to distinguish between systems – equalisation/differentiation, authorised/unauthorised, productive/unproductive – became an important tool for the leadership to identify those systems that needed to be redesigned to drive productive behaviour and activity.

DESIGNING PRODUCTIVE SYSTEMS

How systems are designed and implemented has a significant effect on people's behaviour and consequently how positively viewed and productive an organisation is. As explained, a leader may individually set a great example, but if the systems are unproductive, it will be like swimming against the tide. As a leader, investing in well designed and implemented systems produces far more productive behaviour and activity than attempting to influence individual behaviour alone.

In the example used throughout this chapter, the executive leadership had been unaware of one of the biggest points of leverage for creating a more positively viewed and productive organisation. Once they understood first-hand the relationship between systems design, their own behaviour, and the behaviour being driven in others, and that their organisational systems weren't working as intended, the leadership agreed that designing and implementing more productive systems was required.

It is essential that all systems are executive driven, and this instance was no exception. We took the leadership through the criteria for designing productive systems using a set of questions that needed to be addressed. These questions were used to both critique current systems and design more productive systems:

- Why have you chosen this system to design or redesign?

- How does creating or changing this system support the intention (purpose) of the organisation?

- If you change a system, what are the benefits of the current system and who benefits? E.g., what are you up against?

- What are the boundaries of the system?

- What is the purpose of the system?

- How is the system going to be measured and from whose perspective?

- Is it a system of differentiation or equalisation?

- Who should be the system owner or designer, and have they got the right capability?

- What are the current mythologies (stories) about the system?

- What does the review process look like for assessing whether the system is achieving its purpose and is doing so in the best way?

- How are people rolled into the new system?

- Are the costs of design and implementation understood?

Working through this model, the organisation benefited significantly. Systems were redesigned from being authorised yet unproductive (box B) to become both productive and authorised (box A). Where innovation and improvement had been attempted (box C), these were no longer stifled, and they, too, were redesigned to become both productive and authorised (box A). Where managers used power and overstepped agreed lines of authority (box D), systems were redesigned through a process of understanding and creating role clarity, so that managers had the necessary authority to lead their teams productively (box A).

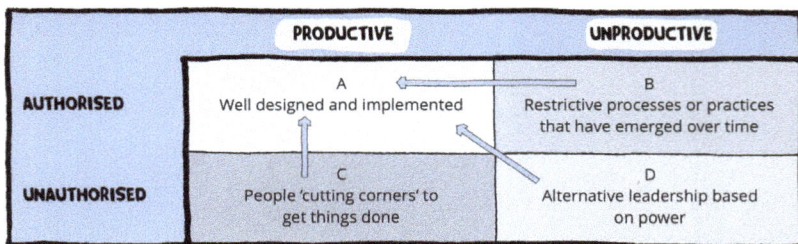

	PRODUCTIVE	UNPRODUCTIVE
AUTHORISED	A Well designed and implemented	B Restrictive processes or practices that have emerged over time
UNAUTHORISED	C People 'cutting corners' to get things done	D Alternative leadership based on power

SYSTEM DESIGN IS ONE OF THE BIGGEST LEVERAGE POINTS FOR IMPROVEMENT IN ANY ORGANISATION

Focusing on designing and implementing productive and authorised organisational systems is a far bigger leverage point for improvement than focusing on the performance of individuals. When people and organisations are liberated from stultifying systems, people are enabled to work more constructively, productively, and creatively, and come to a place of work to willingly contribute to the purpose the organisation has been set up to accomplish.

When this organisation's systems were redesigned and implemented, purpose was better achieved, swathes of unproductive activity disappeared, and operational capacity increased. The constant requests for additional resources ceased. There were significant reductions in unwanted failure demand coming into the contact centre and other channels. Staff engagement scores improved as morale rocketed. Improved financial results followed: operational expenses fell and revenue increased.

After the many failed change programs previously attempted, finally the leadership goals to improve customer service, become more efficient, reduce operational expense, and increase employee engagement were realised. The new productive organisational systems provided the framework to help the organisation turn purpose into a positive and productive day-to-day experience for both customers and employees.

WHAT AM I
MEANT TO DO?

HOW WELL
AM I DOING?

WHAT IS
MY FUTURE?

15
TURNING INTENTION INTO
PRODUCTIVE REALITY

When organisational systems work well and are effective in helping an organisation achieve its purpose, people in the organisation can answer three simple questions:

1. **What am I meant to do?** This question refers to the work of the role and the extent to which someone is clear about the expectations of them, how their work fits with the work others do, and how it contributes to the purpose of the organisation.

2. **How well am I doing?** This question refers to the extent to which the person receives recognition about how they actually achieve those expectations. This does not simply mean comments or information from their manager or supervisor but also feedback from customers and other

stakeholders. How does such feedback match their own experiences and judgement?

3. **What is my future?** This question relates to someone's career and their ambitions (which does not necessarily include promotion). It also refers to information about how the organisation is performing and what future it has.

Using these questions, progressive leaders can determine how clear people are about their current and future work. Typically, in organisations that we have studied, people are unable to answer all three questions. If people cannot answer, or if there is significant ambiguity in their answers, they will not be satisfied in their role and, over time, will become distracted or disengaged from their work.

To create a productive and positively viewed organisation where people can answer these questions with clarity, the coherent integration of the following elements is vital:

Element 1: The work of leadership focuses predominantly on the social domain

Element 2: Using judgement and receiving recognition contributes to positive mental health and identity

Element 3: Complexity in work differs and should be matched to individual capability

Element 4: Turning intention into reality requires individuals to work as a team

The following sections explore what is meant by each of these elements.

ELEMENT 1
THE WORK OF LEADERSHIP FOCUSES PREDOMINANTLY ON THE SOCIAL DOMAIN

There is an assumption that everyone has a shared understanding of the term 'work', but work can be used in many different contexts, such as a place of work, going to work, or having work to do. To ensure a shared understanding, and consistent with our previous statement that any coherent organisational theory has clear definitions, we have defined work as:

Turning intention (purpose) into productive reality.

While undertaking work as defined above undoubtedly requires effort, it is critical to acknowledge that it is not simply the expenditure of effort. In this book, we provide many examples of expenditure of effort which have been unproductive. In any service organisation, everyone is busy, but not everyone is as efficient or effective as they can be. Considerable time, effort, and cost could be saved by liberating people and organisations from stultifying systems (see chapter 14, Liberating people and organisations from stultifying systems), good organisational arrangement (see chapter 17, Designing productive structures), and high-quality leadership. This would release greater capacity and increase the capability of people to concentrate on the work that matters: deliver exceptional services to customers at less cost, and create positive, productive places to work.

The work required to create a successful organisation can be categorised into three distinct domains:

- a **technical** domain, which reflects activity relating to the knowledge and skills that are applied to tasks that help achieve the purpose of an organisation

- a **commercial** domain, which can be described as the activity relating to costs, revenue, capital – in short, value for money

- a **social** domain, which consists of all the activity needed to allow people to work together

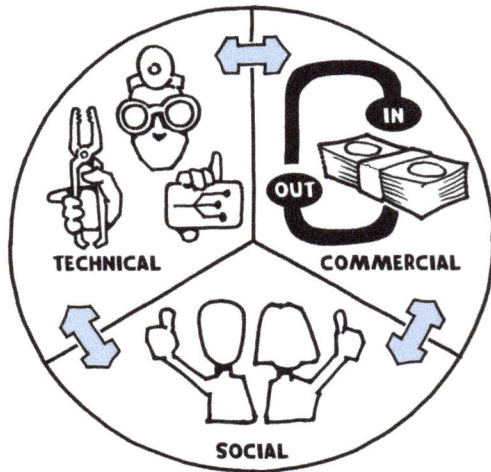

Work completed in each domain must be integrated for the organisation to achieve its purpose. It is important not to elevate any domain above another, but to acknowledge that roles within an organisation require people to do different types of work of equal importance. With this context, the work of leadership focuses predominantly on the social domain, which includes social processes. Social process is defined as person-to-person interaction. The effectiveness of a leader's social process skills will have an impact on how successful they are in their leadership work. A leader needs to be able to observe the behaviour of others and comprehend how this behaviour does, or does not, contribute to a productive outcome. The impact of a leader's skills in social processes is significant – most likely you or someone you know may have left an organisation because of poor leadership, and, clearly, organisations cannot afford to lose talent. We have found that focusing on increasing capability within the social domain leads not only to improved satisfaction of employees but, even more importantly, to improved outcomes for customers.

ELEMENT 2
USING JUDGEMENT AND RECEIVING RECOGNITION CONTRIBUTES TO POSITIVE MENTAL HEALTH AND IDENTITY

In our experience when people speak about work, and when they assign worth to their work, they value the ability to use their judgement and discretion when they turn intention into reality. In other words, motivation for people is intrinsic. Ironically, motivation does not occur through the many traditional extrinsic schemes that are employed.

It is a leader's role to create the conditions where an individual can exercise their judgement and discretion: creating an environment where people willingly come to work and positively, creatively, and productively contribute to delivering the purpose the organisation has been set up to accomplish.

We have found that every leader we talk to or work with recognises that they hire people to make good decisions and do productive work. So, at least in theory, there is a common goal between leaders and the people they employ. However, in reality, and despite the large body of literature on delegation, leaders grapple with the dissonance between allowing people to use their judgement and the risks of poor decision making. Leaders often point out that they are ultimately the ones who are held accountable for decisions taken by their teams. This is true, and this dissonance should not be ignored. However, the leader should resist the urge to retreat into a less complicated world and, instead, recognise the complexity and embrace this dissonance. The alternative is to become overly reliant on standard processes and complicated compliance regimes and become overly risk averse and outsource their leadership to external parties such as HR and Risk teams. This response will result in red tape (detailed policies, systems, processes, and rules) that predictably create inefficiency, unsatisfying jobs, high turnover, and a work-to-rule culture.

The first step to creating the conditions where an individual can exercise judgement and discretion is to help leaders see first-hand that the systems that surround their team members are not well designed and productive. If people are prevented by organisational systems from using judgement and discretion, their mental health suffers, as well as their sense of identity. Once leaders design and implement productive systems, employees light up. People who work in a well-designed system can use judgement and discretion, are enabled to improve the way their work is done, are free to work productively to their potential, and can use technology that complements their work, enhances cognitive processes, and automates simple and repetitive tasks. In such a workplace, work becomes more satisfying and creative, efficiency improves, and both costs and risk decrease.

The second step to creating the conditions where an individual can exercise their judgement and discretion is to help leaders see that if people feel someone is telling them 'how to turn intention into reality' (that is, how to do their job) or if they do not get recognition for their contribution, their engagement with the work will also be negatively impacted. This behaviour is simply poor leadership and will ultimately contradict or undermine any work to implement a productive organisational system.

It is the job of leadership to build individual capability to ensure good decisions are made. To build this capability, it is helpful for a leader first to clarify for individuals what needs to be achieved, and why. Therefore, it is critical for a leader to engage with people and be clear about the purpose, the context of the work, and constraints. Research[63] has shown the importance of having a clear understanding of shared purpose (intention) and its impact on motivation and well-being in collectively working to achieve that purpose.

---

63   See, e.g., 'Why business must harness the power of purpose', EY Global, Dec 2020.

Once the what and why are clarified, the how can be developed. This is where leaders need to build capability in others to ensure good decisions are made. The how is all about people exercising judgement and discretion within a set of known constraints that provide the context for the use of discretion. These outcomes may be simple and visible, such as answering a customer phone call, or they may be more abstract and complex, such as implementing a digital strategy throughout a large organisation. Regardless, work is always going to be bounded by some constraints, such as the laws set out by society, the policies of an organisation, the authority as defined by a role, available resources, and generally a set time frame.

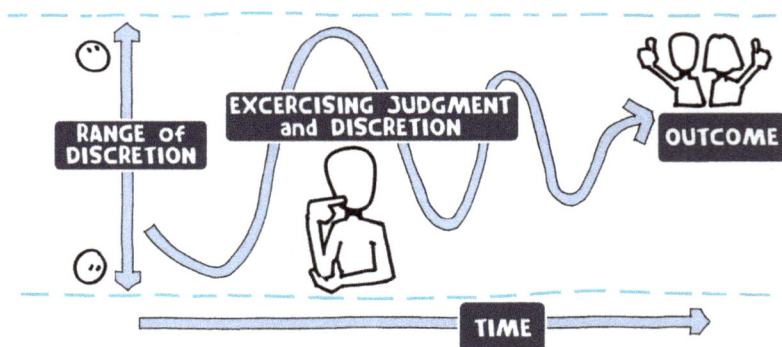

Importantly, the how is and should be unique to an individual. To feel positive about work, it is important for people to always feel that they have control over the how. When people feel positive about their work, they are intrinsically motivated. They are more likely to acknowledge the quality of performance and be willing to receive recognition for that work. Providing recognition (both positive and negative) is an important and authentic element of leadership if leaders seek to grow another person's capability. Consequently, we regard the recognition of work as essential to mental health and identity.

ELEMENT 3
COMPLEXITY IN WORK DIFFERS AND SHOULD BE MATCHED TO INDIVIDUAL CAPABILITY

In Element 1, we talked about the importance of clarifying what work is. We also recognised that not all work is the same. Depending on context, individuals complete work that is focused in either the technical, commercial, or social domain to contribute to the achievement of the organisation's purpose. Additionally, work will differ in terms of complexity. In Element 2, we showed that being able to use judgement and discretion is a vital component for an individual to productively turn intention into reality, and stressed the importance for people to receive recognition for their effort in doing work in the context of mental health and identity. The third element, explored here, looks at individual capability and matching this to the differing levels of complexity of work an organisation must complete to achieve its purpose.

First, people need to be aware of their current and future capability in order to complete their work productively. It is a vital part of a leader's role to understand and recognise an individual's current capability. This understanding forms the basis to develop capability into the future. But how do we define individual capability? The combination of the following features forms our definition of individual capability:

Knowledge: People gain capability from the knowledge they gather over time.

Skills: The ability to apply the knowledge they have gained.

Social Process Skills: The ability to understand and manage social processes (the way that people behave and work together).

Mental Processing Ability: The way an individual organises their thinking when working (attempting to turn intention into reality).

Application: The effort and energy that a person puts into applying the other elements of capability to their work.

We have excluded tenure/experience and personality/temperament from the definition of individual capability. This is deliberate, because we have found that these factors can be deceptive. For example, a person's capability based on tenure assumes a person's experience automatically translates into increased capability, which is a flawed assumption. We can all likely think of someone who was promoted beyond their capability or was transferred to a 'special project' because of their lack of capability, or situations where people are unable to progress until someone above them retires.

Likewise, linking personality or temperament to capability can be misleading. There are some very successful introverted leaders that do not fit the stereotypical charismatic style of leadership. Equally, we can all think of very charismatic people who turned out to be awful leaders. Research and our experience have shown that the combination of the five features (knowledge, skills, social processing skills, mental processing ability and application) define individual capability.[64]

Work and individual capability now have clear definitions, but what about the concept of differing levels of complexity in work? Generally, work is completed as a series of tasks. Some of those tasks are more complex than others. For example, some tasks will require a person to think in a 10-year time frame, while others will require people to think only in terms of what they do tomorrow. Subsequently, productive organisations require people with different capabilities to work with, and make sense of, the varying

---

64 See, e.g., Systems Leadership: Creating Positive Organisations, Macdonald, Burke and Stewart, p. 86.

complexity created by tasks of differing time spans. Remember, this is not about experience or IQ; it's about the capability to deal with differing levels of ambiguity, complexity, and abstraction.

Capability can be increased over time through gaining more knowledge or developing new skills to apply that knowledge. Additionally, improving social process skills, such as listening, can help people be better leaders or improve how leaders work with other people. After all, a positive environment helps people apply themselves at work.

However, there is one ability that does not improve over time in the same way as the other capabilities – our mental processing ability. Research has proven our ability to make order out of disorder, and handling ambiguity, complexity, and abstraction ceases to develop once we reach adulthood.[65] Therefore, although people can acquire knowledge, learn new skills, and put in effort and energy to realise their potential, this same improvement does not occur in their capability in dealing with complexity.

These findings impact on matching complexity to capability in the workplace. It means an organisation needs a mix of people operating at differing levels of complexity, so that it has the capabilities required to cope with the variation in the work an organisation must complete to achieve its purpose.

---

65   See, e.g., Systems Leadership, Macdonald, Burke and Stewart, p. 93.

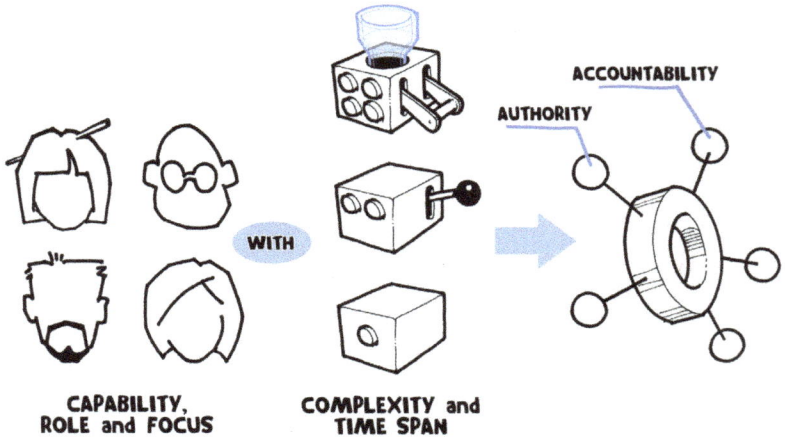

CAPABILITY, ROLE and FOCUS   **COMPLEXITY and TIME SPAN**

Organisationally, if someone is tasked to work at a level where their capability does not match the complexity of the role, that individual becomes stressed, and it often causes them to act defensively and affect their ability to effectively carry out tasks required of the role. For example, promoting the best class teacher to the school principal role might not work, as there is a greater level of complexity in the principal's role. If leaders mismatch capability and complexity, not only is this a source of stress for the individual but it can also lead to confusion and, at worst, cynicism towards the way the organisation is structured and managed. Conversely, if capability and complexity are well matched for people, that organisation is well on the way to being able to turn its intention into productive reality.

ELEMENT 4
TURNING INTENTION INTO REALITY REQUIRES INDIVIDUALS TO WORK AS A TEAM

Each of the three elements described thus far are essential for leaders to create an environment of clarity where people willingly come to work and positively, creatively, and productively contribute to delivering the purpose the organisation has been set up to accomplish.

When people are clear about their work, can improve their own work, can use judgement and discretion and receive recognition, and are in roles that match their capability to the complexity of the work, they are more engaged and satisfied in their role. Work becomes more productive, fulfilling, and positively viewed.

The focus of this chapter has been on creating the conditions where an individual can thrive. However, a large part of work involves a social process, that is, the interaction of individuals to achieve a purpose. In an organisation, this interaction usually happens within a team. A team is defined as:

☑ A group of people, including a leader, with a common purpose who must interact with each other to achieve that purpose.

An important element of this definition is the need to interact; without this, they are just a group of people who do not share a purpose. In other words, a group is not always a team.

Clearly, a team needs to work well together if an organisation is to achieve its purpose. That is, they need to exhibit *productive teamwork*. This requires specific work to be completed by both the leader and team members.

PRODUCTIVE TEAM LEADERSHIP

Let's start with the leader. There are leaders of teams throughout an organisational hierarchy. A CEO leads a team of executives, an executive leads a team of department heads, a department head leads senior managers, and so on. For each level of leadership, their work begins with setting context. This requires the leader to explain the situation the team is currently in – a leader should never assume that the context is understood. Clarifying the context is an opportunity for the leader to create a mutual understanding of the constraints that the team must work within. We often see lack of context as a major inhibitor to productive work.

Once the context has been explained and mutually understood, the leader needs to clearly articulate a statement of purpose. This could be the purpose of a task, project, meeting, or basically anything else that requires a mutual understanding of what the team are there to do.

Following the establishment of a shared understanding of context and purpose, the leader needs to consider what issue(s) will stop the achievement of purpose. These issues need to be critical ones, and a useful way of identifying critical issues is to pause and consider: Does this issue need to be thought about and worked on? If the answer is no, then the issue is more than likely to be a known constraint.

Most leaders require contributions from others to identify these critical issues. This inclusive process is an important element of leadership and engages the team. There is a risk to any leader who, instead, chooses to go it alone. Not only can this alienate a team but it also increases the risk that the leader will miss something important.

Once these critical issues have been identified, it is the leader's responsibility to create a plan to address them. If sufficient effort is made to genuinely seek contribution from the team, the plan will have a much better chance of being accepted. Ultimately, the leader will be accountable for the outcome of the plan, both in concrete terms and how people experience the creation of the plan. Sometimes they can develop it on their own, but most of the time the leader will seek contribution. While seeking contribution is not a prerequisite, it is an example of a good use of social process.

Careful consideration needs to be given to the integration of contributions to the plan, and if someone's contribution has not been included in the plan, they need to know why. It is important to note that consensus may not be achieved – consensus is not the aim of this process. What is important is that the individuals within the team feel they have been heard and the plan addresses the issues they think will prevent them from achieving a purpose.

The plan will be broken down into a series of tasks. The team must know what the tasks are, who is completing them, how the tasks integrate with other tasks, how the task will be measured, and how the tasks help with the achievement of purpose. It is the leader's role to provide this clarity. Importantly, if a leader is assigning a task, they must acknowledge the capability of the individual assigned to deal with the complexity of work required. This acknowledgement has a bearing on how successful a person will be in completing the task. Even if someone in a team is self-assigning a task, they need to be aware of their capability and the inherent complexity of the task. Equally important is the shared understanding that the path chosen to complete the task (the how) is up to the individual completing the work.

Finally, it is also the leader's role to monitor and review this process. What we have described as good team leadership is fundamentally based on the use of social processes. As such, it is vital for the leader to observe and comprehend the impact on the social cohesion of the team. Social cohesion helps engender good work performance and should be worked on constantly. In this context, the leader should be wary of the following traps:

1. **Being over involved in the how** – If a leader struggles to add value to the work of others, they will seek other work to do. This invariably means the leader is doing the work of others and overly involved with someone else's how.

2. **Dropping down into the level of complexity below their role** – If a leader is unable to deal with the complexity of their role, they will seek out work that suits their capability. (This, unfortunately, and invariably, leads to the first trap.)

3. **Being the technical expert** – The leader behaves as though they must know more than anyone else in the team. Superior knowledge and expertise are often mistaken for leadership by those who seek to demonstrate it.

4. **Feeling they have to have the answer** – The leader feels a failure for not being able to generate the complete solution personally or for saying, 'I don't know'.

5. **Treating every issue as critical** – A leader has a laundry list of problems to solve, because they struggle with ambiguity, complexity, and abstraction. To them, everything looks critical.

6. **Not being a leader** – Team leadership is not designed as a democracy. As such, sometimes a leader is required to make a decision that does not reflect the consensus among the group. A good leader does not shy away from the situation.

This is not an exhaustive list, but it encompasses the most common traps leaders need to avoid when they are creating and improving social cohesion within a team.

PRODUCTIVE TEAM MEMBERSHIP

Whilst team leaders have responsibilities as we've outlined above, it is just as important to recognise the responsibilities that team members have in creating social cohesion within the team.

A team member must take responsibility for ensuring they understand context and purpose. If a person does not understand something, they must ask a question. Remember, there is no such thing as a stupid question! The chances are that if it is unclear to one person, it will be unclear to others.

When asked for contributions, the team member has work to do. Saying nothing either signifies there is nothing to say or agreement to what is being said. A team member may think that their point is trivial, but it could also be critical and being missed by the leader. If there is a good social process, it should be safe to have open and wide-ranging discussions about issues that could derail the team's efforts.

Equally as important as contributing is to listen to others and resist the urge to close others down. Really listening is hard work – it is an active, not passive, process and must show the other person that they are truly being heard.

Once the context and purpose are understood, and everybody has had the opportunity to contribute to identifying any issues, it is the leader's role to create a plan of action. At this stage, it is the responsibility of the team member to accept the leader's decision as to which plan will be actioned. If the team member has had a fair opportunity to contribute, it is their responsibility to commit to this chosen pathway.

The plan will have a series of tasks, and the team member is now required to ensure that they understand the following:

- What is the purpose of the task?

- How will the task be measured?

- How does the task contribute to the plan?

- How does the task fit with what others are doing?

If a team member is not sure about any of the above, they should seek clarification. Being a productive team member is an active process, not a matter of blind faith. The principle is: *If in doubt, ask!*

Finally, it is a responsibility of the team member to co-operate and collaborate with colleagues and accept coaching from others.

Social cohesion will help engender good teamwork and should be worked on constantly. In this context, team members need to be wary of the following traps:

1. **Keeping quiet** – This infers that either you have nothing to say or that you agree with what is being done. It is best to be active, rather than passive, in this situation.

2. **Not listening to others** – Listening is an active process and is an important social process skill. Active listening shows

other people you are interested, and this helps create social cohesion within a group.

3. **'See? I knew I was right!'** – If you have not contributed or actively listened to colleagues, you have not shown good team member behaviour. As such, you relinquish the opportunity to criticise the decisions made by the leader and team. This type of behaviour is usually an exercise of power to undermine and destabilise the team and leadership.

4. **Holding back because you might upset the leader** – Holding back comes from a fear of taking over. As long as a person exhibits good social process, this should be manageable. A bigger problem would be keeping quiet and not expressing a view.

CREATING CLARITY LEADS TO A PRODUCTIVE ORGANISATION

We started this chapter by stating the importance of creating clarity for individuals in a work context. If an individual does not understand what they do, how they are measured, and what the future looks like, they will not be satisfied in their role and will become distracted or disengaged from their work over time.

We provided a clear definition for work – *turning intention into reality* – and looked at work across the three domains: technical, commercial, and social, acknowledging that no domain is of greater importance than another; it is just different work. We identified that, in a productive organisation, the work of leadership focuses predominantly on the social domain.

We emphasised the importance of people to be able to exercise judgement and discretion in systems that are well designed and productive. When this happens, people become intrinsically motivated. As such, they positively identify with their work and are more likely to receive recognition for their effort. It is a leader's role to give that recognition. Additionally, it falls to the leader to create an understanding of the constraints that apply to the use of judgement and discretion. This understanding allows a person to create a pathway (the how) to complete their work. As we have noted, a leader must ensure they remove themselves from the how, unless specifically asked to contribute. The how must remain unique to the person completing the work.

We also discussed that not all work in an organisation is the same. Work differs based on task complexity. Critically, that means an organisation needs a mix of people operating at differing levels of complexity. This mix ensures the right people with the right capabilities occupy roles that can cope with the variation in the work an organisation must complete to achieve its purpose. When capability and complexity are well matched, an organisation is well on the way to being able to turn intention into productive reality.

We have also recognised that individuals do not operate in isolation – most work is completed as part of a team. Consequently, the way people work together has a great bearing on how well an organisation achieves its purpose. We have outlined the processes for both productive team leadership and team membership. These processes are designed to achieve clarity and coherence between a team leader and member(s). Teamwork is an essential component of a productive and positively viewed organisation. It is the heartbeat of the human interaction, or social process, within an organisation. Achieving effective teamwork is complex and ongoing work, but it is also immensely rewarding and critical to achieve the organisation's purpose. In short, creating clarity for individuals within teams creates social cohesion, which, in turn, creates a positively viewed and productive organisation.

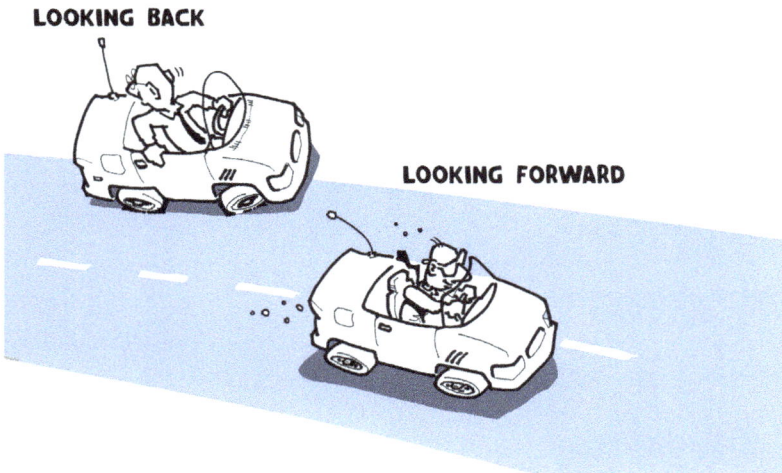

LOOKING BACK

LOOKING FORWARD

16
ARE YOU RUNNING YOUR ORGANISATION THROUGH THE REAR-VIEW MIRROR?

When designing and implementing productive organisational systems, it is critical to agree on how each system is going to be measured. A cohesive system of measurement ensures that each system contributes to the organisation's purpose, and does so in the best possible way.

The caveat with all measurement systems and/or measures is that they drive behaviour. This is why it is particularly important that the measures are valid and the leader knows both the behaviour the measures drive and what systems surround the measure. Measures must explicitly link to an individual's work, and the impact on behaviour must be understood.

There is a systemic relationship between purpose, measures, and work. The following diagram illustrates the relationship between these elements.

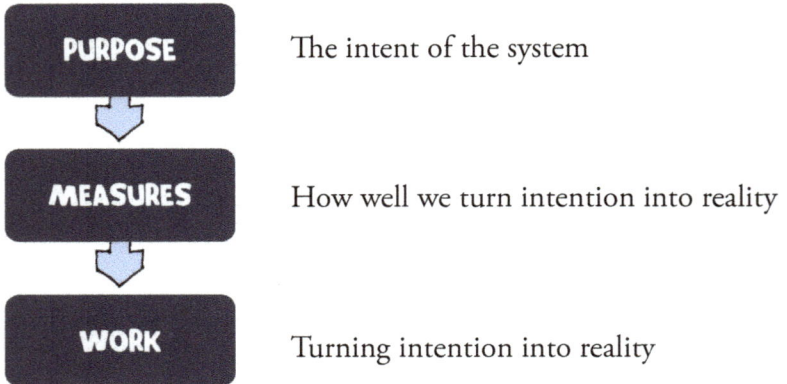

PURPOSE	The intent of the system
MEASURES	How well we turn intention into reality
WORK	Turning intention into reality

Choosing a measure or measurement system that drives unproductive behaviour and activity is a serious leadership error. Rather than starting with a purpose defined from the intent of a system, it is a common error to unintentionally create a de facto purpose to 'make the numbers'. For example, people are told to focus on making the numbers, such as individual performance targets, incentives, work states, and/or conformance to standards. A singular focus on making the numbers either caps performance or drives unproductive behaviour and activity, or both, because work is undertaken with the sole intent to make the boss happy, and maybe reap a financial or other type of reward.

Leaders pay attention to things which (rightly or wrongly) matter to them – and what they pay attention to gets done. The more people focus on making their numbers, the less they focus on achieving the purpose the organisation has been set up to accomplish. The following diagram illustrates how this relationship often operates in practice.

MEASURES	Targets, incentives, work-states, standards
⬇	
PURPOSE	'Make the numbers'
⬇	
WORK	Unproductive behaviour and activity

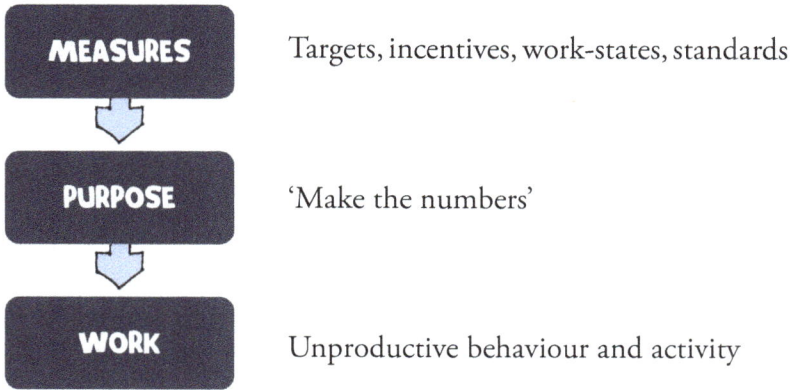

The above diagram demonstrates a contingent relationship, that is, a relationship where 'If you do this, then you get that'. What this type of relationship does is cause the person to focus on the 'you get that', rather than focusing on achieving the purpose the organisation has been set up to accomplish. The same problem applies to incentive-based pay systems; when leaders make things contingent with pay, they devalue the work and people start valuing the prize. The outcomes noted in chapter 13 from the Australian Banking Royal Commission are a perfect example of how contingent-based individual targets and remuneration systems drove unproductive behaviour and activity. We described further examples in chapter 13, What drives unproductive behaviour and activity?

Many leaders are obsessed with managing another number – cost – but counterintuitively, a focus on driving costs down actually forces costs up. Here are two examples. Limiting the time call centre workers spend on calls (reduced cost per call) means that customers often don't get their problems solved and are forced to call again (increased overall cost). And targeting repairers with the number of jobs per day (reduced cost per job), means that jobs are not completed in one visit, instead requiring second or third visits to complete (increased overall cost). Managing this way fools leaders into believing they are successful – the numbers are being met – but they cannot see what is really happening. When leaders can see the total cost to the organisation, and discover that their current approaches to performance management actually ignore the reality of performance, they realise that focusing on achieving purpose drives costs down. So, in these examples, ensuring more customer calls are resolved at the first point of transaction drives costs down, and ensuring more repairs are completed on the first visit drives costs down too.

Organisational systems should be designed to be productive, to achieve a purpose, and in doing so, drive productive behaviour and activity. All measures in a system drive behaviour. It is important that measures are valid and that the leader knows both the behaviour the measure drives and what systems surround the measure. The measure must be explicitly linked to the individual's work, and the linkage to behaviour must be understood. The fundamental relationships to be understood are the interactions between:

1. how well purpose is operationalised

2. how well the measures are designed to drive productive behaviour and activity

3. how well work achieves the purpose the organisation has been set up to accomplish

DEVELOPING A LEADING MEASURE

It is a truism that we have to have measures, but not all measures are good. In a service organisation, we need measures that give us insight into how well we understand and deliver the things that achieve purpose. Very few, if any, conventional measures are born out of that perspective. Typically, what is measured are things that leaders will have judged and assumed to be important; for example, performance targets, budgets, work states, service levels, activity, objectives, incentives and so on. We classify these as *arbitrary measures*, that is, a standard that someone has arbitrarily set as a measure of success or failure.

In addition to these arbitrary measures, leaders also use what we call *lagging measures*. Customer satisfaction, staff morale, and all financial measures are examples of lagging measures. Whilst these are not arbitrary measures, lagging measures only tell leaders what has happened and will never help them understand why.

Instead of using arbitrary and lagging measures, there is a better set of measures leaders can use to understand how well work achieves the purpose the organisation has been set up to accomplish. These alternative measures are what we call *leading measures*, which show the capability to achieve purpose.

For example, when a customer makes a claim, we need to establish measures for how long it takes to settle a claim from first contact until settlement. Another example is when a customer needs something to be repaired; it would be useful to establish measures of how frequently a job is completed on the first visit. Both examples help an organisation establish how well they deliver on their purpose.

What we find, though, when working in service organisations is that it is common for people to try and make the numbers look right. Using the claims service example above, it's not uncommon for the clock to start only when all claim information is received from the customer, and for the clock to stop while waiting for further information from customers. In a repairs service organisation, it's not uncommon for a repair to be recorded as complete when, in actuality, more work is required in a subsequent visit.

To develop a leading measure, the principle is: *Leading measures should demonstrate achievement of purpose.* It means finding out how well intention is turned into reality, and working on any issues as the sources of improvement. Knowing *why* something happens (leading) is more important than knowing *that* something has happened (lagging).

REACTING TO GOOD OR BAD NUMBERS

Once new leading measures are defined, leaders have better measures of performance, but the problem becomes one of how to interpret the data. Numbers are the lifeblood of management decisions, but the quality of resulting decisions depends on whether numbers illuminate or obscure how well work achieves purpose.

People typically look at data in terms of its variance. We live in a world where we have been taught to think about variance. It is in all of the management literature, and is how leaders have learned to judge performance. Variance assumes difference from something; for example, the achieved number differs from a forecasted number or target.

Leaders focus on the extent to which the number differs, and based on whether it is good or bad, react accordingly. People have to justify performance (often in the form of a report or email) because of a perceived decline based on a few data points. It is quite normal for a leader, for instance, to look at two measures of output and treat the numbers as though they tell different stories. It may be that if the first number is high, it is equated to being good, and people receive a pat on the back. The second number may be low, which is judged as bad, and people are told to pull their socks up and explain. When the next number is higher, the leader feels gratified that their intervention has obviously had the desired effect. But what if this variation were typical, only to be expected from normal performance?

LOOKING AT DATA DIFFERENTLY

Typically, numbers are shown in reports; for example, pie charts, histograms, tabular data, and performance indicators. These reports are all static and historical (a picture of past performance) and not dynamic.

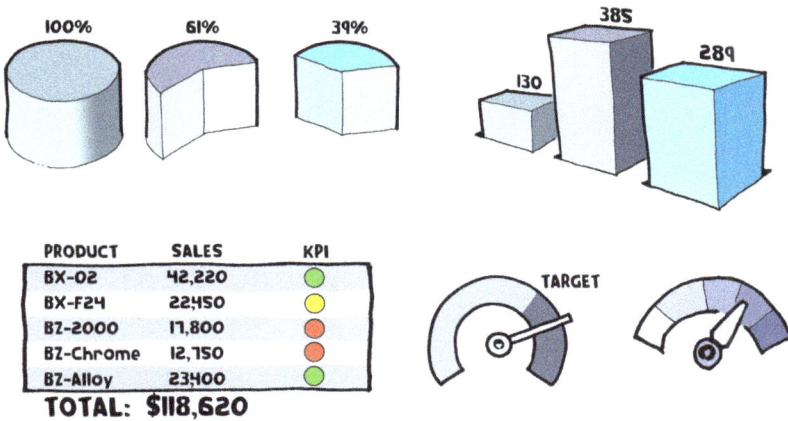

PRODUCT	SALES	KPI
BX-02	42,220	🟢
BX-F24	22,450	🟡
BZ-2000	17,800	🟠
BZ-Chrome	12,750	🟠
BZ-Alloy	23,400	🟢

TOTAL: $118,620

In many organisations, reporting this data has become a self-sustaining industry, with an army of people spending much of their time filling in and compiling reports in documents, spreadsheets, and slide packs, the only certain result being the consumption of an incredible amount of resources and time.

Why do people use reports and data such as the above? Because it is all so normal that it is rarely questioned. However, normal doesn't necessarily mean good or useful. To move beyond the limitations of normal practice, a leader must understand the concept of variation and recognise its implications for performance management.

THE THEORY OF VARIATION

W. Edwards Deming pointed out there are two significant mistakes made in how leaders have been taught to understand and use performance numbers:[66]

1. Taking action when they shouldn't

2. Not taking action when they should

As a leader, the only way to not make these mistakes is to look at data differently, and to do so requires applying the four principles of variation theory to measures and measurement systems:

Principle 1: We should expect things to vary; they always do

Principle 2: Understanding variation tells us what to expect

Principle 3: Understanding variation leads to improvement

Principle 4: Understanding variation tells us when there has been a genuine change in performance

PRINCIPLE 1: WE SHOULD EXPECT THINGS TO VARY; THEY ALWAYS DO

The first principle of the theory of variation is that we should expect things to vary. They always do. Instead of static data in the form of histograms, pie charts, and the like, to better understand capability we can plot numbers into a chart, which helps us understand variation in performance.

---

66   See, e.g., 'Impact of Process Tampering on Variation', The W. Edwards Deming Institute, 14 Jan 2019.

Let's look at a simple example. In the following chart we have plotted how long it takes someone to get to work over a period of 14 days.

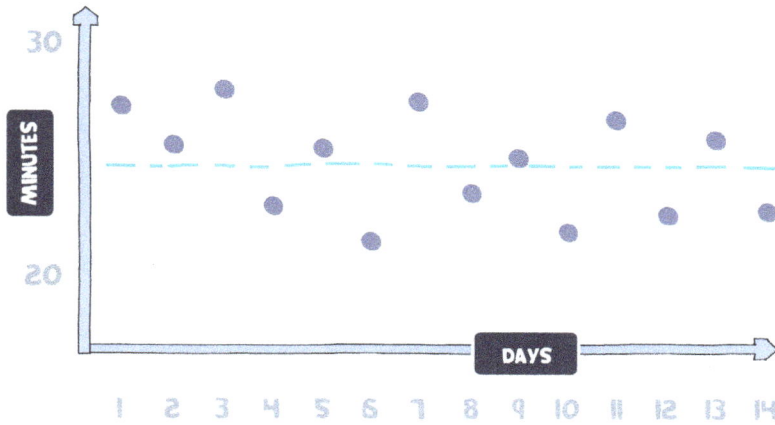

Chart 1: Daily commute time

The chart shows variation in their commute. On day one, the travel time was 27 minutes, day two it was 26 minutes, day three 28 minutes, and so on.

There will be different factors that affect their journey time. This seems logical and obvious. There is natural and inherent variation in any system. Therefore, what seems logical when applied to travelling to work should also seem logical when applied to other measures that we use when we are at work. Sadly, though, it is not.

Everybody knows that any organisation is buffeted by all manner of factors, internal and external; thus, the performance of its services and the organisation as a whole is subject to variation. A look at any performance numbers will always show ups and downs, some seemingly better than others, which seem worse. However, if, over time, the ups and downs remain consistent, that is, they all remain within a consistent range of variation, that reflects the stable state, and enables people to more accurately predict future performance. This approach is discussed in the next section.

PRINCIPLE 2: UNDERSTANDING VARIATION TELLS US WHAT TO EXPECT

Understanding variation helps leaders to learn what to expect. Walter Shewhart created what are called control charts.[67] He showed that by using a basic statistical formula, people can see whether variation is predictable or unpredictable.

Taking the daily commute time data we used in chart 1, chart 2 shows that the journey time into work is perfectly predictable. Why? Because the travel time per day is between what is known as the upper control limit (UCL) and the lower control limit (LCL).

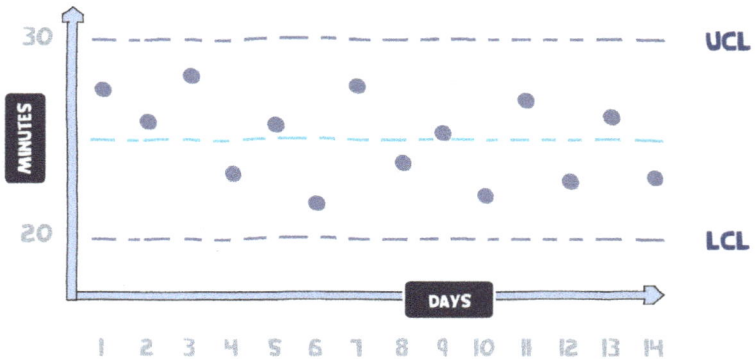

Chart 2: Daily commute time control chart

The technicalities of how these limits are calculated are explained in detail by Wheeler.[68] However, suffice to say, the upper and lower limits are set by the natural variation in the data. If the points plotted lie between the upper and lower limits, then the variation is predictable and in control; in other words, a number near the bottom is just as likely to happen as a number at the top. It's not that the numbers are good or bad; it simply means that

---

67   See, Control Chart, American Society for Quality.

68   Wheeler, D. J. & Chambers, D. S., *Understanding Statistical Process Control*, Knoxville, TN: SPC Press, 1992.

this is the variation that occurs naturally. The chart shows that for the journey into work, it is just as likely to take the person 20 minutes (the lower end) as it is to take them 30 minutes (the upper end), with the average being 25 minutes.

The chart also shows that it would be a mistake to predict their journey time based on the average. Most of us are taught to think about numbers as averages. Average numbers will be in all our reports and they appear in our daily lives in circumstances such as the average train punctuality displayed at train stations or average pick-up times for an Uber or taxi. However, averages hide actual performance. Someone might see the average pick-up time for a taxi is 3 mins 57 seconds and think, hang on, I didn't get picked up in that time! We intuitively know that not everyone receives the average, and yet we still use averages everywhere as a measure of success or failure. Using chart 2, how many times did the person experience the average commute time of 25 minutes? The answer is none, yet averages are the lifeblood of many organisational measures.

If performance is predictable and in control, what would be the impact of setting a target time of 25 minutes (based on the average) for getting to work? As performance is predictable, it is clear that no one can expect to reach that target every time.

Targets do not incorporate an understanding of variation; instead, they either cap performance or drive unproductive behaviour and activity in order to make the numbers. An example of this is when leaders set targets and standards for on-time percentage performance for train services. They proudly display performance of the current period versus the last (variance thinking in action) but are unaware of the consequences. These kinds of numbers put a limit, or a ceiling, on performance. People learn to work to the target or standard and not go beyond it; alternatively, they work out how to game the system. For example, train operators adjust the timetables so the train could be late but still appear to be on time, or if the target doesn't apply if the train doesn't run, train operators cancel trains. A better approach would be to understand current performance and work out how it can be improved. This is what we discuss next.

PRINCIPLE 3: UNDERSTANDING VARIATION LEADS TO IMPROVEMENT

Planning requires prediction. Charting data in control charts helps people see what is predictably being achieved and becomes a more effective basis for managing and planning.

When you look at data this way, there are only two types of performance numbers shown in the chart: common numbers and special numbers. To illustrate the difference between common and special, let's take the example of the person traveling to work. We've established that it predictably takes the person between 20 and 30 minutes to travel to work – any numbers within this range are *common* performance numbers. They are typical and predictable, and variation exists in these numbers because of the system design. The other type of performance numbers is *special*, which arises from something happening to the system. For example, if there were a fault on the train line and it took an hour to get to work, this is a special performance number, but we know what caused it, and it can be ignored (it's just 'noise'). However, if their journey time consistently took longer, then why these special performance numbers were occurring would be useful to understand, a signal to investigate further.

Unfortunately, leaders often behave as if common and special performance numbers are one and the same. As soon as something 'different' occurs, they react and end up taking action when they shouldn't, or not taking action when they should, just like Deming observed.

Control charts provide a window to performance and help people to ask different and better questions, but as Deming stated: 'The control chart is no substitute for the brain'.[69]

---

69 Deming, W. E., *Elementary Principles of the Statistical Control of Quality*, Tokyo: Nippon Kagaku Gijutsu Renmei, 1951, p. 69.

PRINCIPLE 4: UNDERSTANDING VARIATION TELLS US WHEN THERE HAS BEEN A GENUINE CHANGE IN PERFORMANCE

Instead of causing people to react to predictable ups and downs, control charts help people to understand when there has been a genuine change in performance. Let's look at a real-life example. A local authority runs a housing benefits service. If a person were out of work and needed help to pay their rent, they would approach the local authority. What matters to the person seeking help is that a decision is made and money is paid to them before their next rent payment is due. The starting point for improvement is to understand how long the service predictably takes to help people.

As is common in most service organisations, if leaders want to know how much it costs to do a certain activity, that number is easily obtained. However, if they want to determine how long it takes a customer to get what they want – from their very first point of contact with the organisation through to when their demand was resolved – that question is often much harder to answer. In this local authority example, the data had to be gathered manually and placed in a control chart. Chart 3 illustrates performance over time. The x-axis is the date the claims started and the y-axis is the number of days it took to settle the claims. The data showed that, predictably, someone claiming help could expect their claim to be settled anywhere between two and 160 days. It was a shock to senior leaders when a true reflection of performance from a customer's point of view was understood.

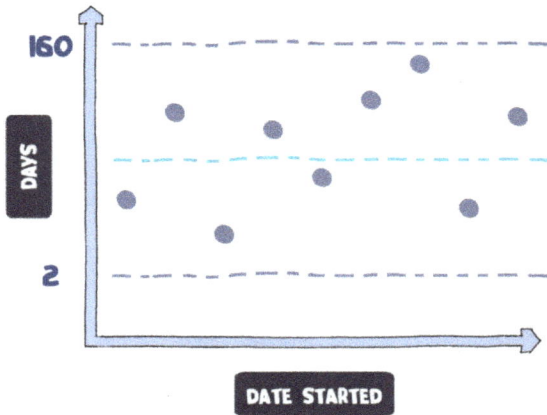

Chart 3: The number of days to settle a claim

The organisation set about redesigning the service using the following steps:

1. Determine what creates value for people claiming and how best to service them, and use that information to set the context for improvement

2. Organise and enable people to deliver outcomes more effectively, supported by productive organisational systems and structures

3. And, only then, apply the minimum required technology that complements the more effective organisational systems and structures, enhances cognitive processes, and automates simple and repetitive tasks

This three-step approach enabled the organisation to achieve improved claim resolution outcomes in just a matter of weeks. A genuine improvement in performance is shown in chart 4. There, the data has been split at the point where there was a new trend in performance numbers, which was a result of the new systems and structures being put in place. The chart shows that someone claiming help could now expect that help to be delivered in a maximum of 10 days, a massive improvement.

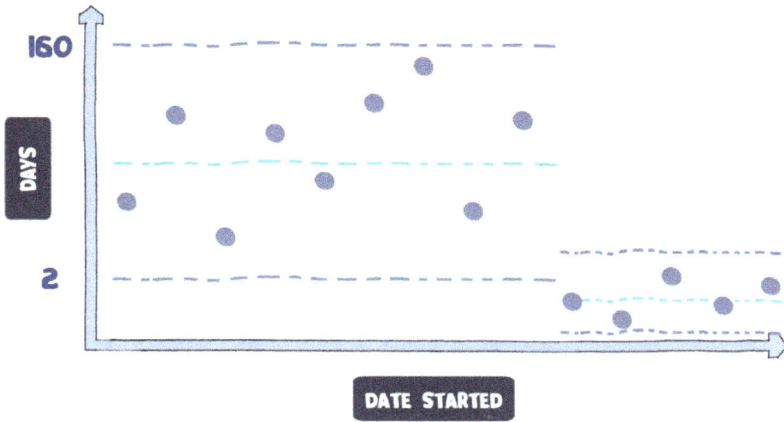

Chart 4: A genuine improvement in the number of days to settle a claim

Variation in performance is inherent, but reducing the range of variation drives costs down and improves performance. As in the housing benefits service, once the causes of variation are known, they can be worked on so that the organisation is more productive and service delivery is improved.

FOCUS ON LEADING MEASURES AND IMPROVEMENT IN LAGGING MEASURES WILL FOLLOW

As we have shown, paying attention to lagging and arbitrary measures only gives leaders the illusion of control. These measures can only tell leaders what has happened, and never helps them understand why. Leaders are, as Deming put it, running their organisation through the rear-view mirror. By contrast, leading measures result in real control: helping leaders to understand how well work achieves the purpose the organisation has been set up to accomplish.

An example of the benefits of gaining real control through the use of leading measures is provided by Danik Lucas, an executive at WorkCover Queensland. He recounts the results achieved at WorkCover Queensland when he and his leadership team redesigned their measurement system:

> 66 *We've realised that numbers only tell part of the story and that we had to look deeper to understand how well work achieved the purpose the organisation has been set up to accomplish.*
>
> *We now pay closer attention to leading measures. We work with the data to actually understand variation and what it is telling us. We focus on observing the work to understand performance and to understand what's important to customers.*
>
> *We now have a very strong lens for knowing whether we deliver what matters to customers and if people experience their work positively.*

Once leading measures are defined, all arbitrary measures can be designed out and any current organisation-wide lagging measures can assume a subordinate role in decision making. Of course, effort and method are required to systematically replace and eliminate arbitrary measures currently linked to roles, review systems, remuneration systems, procedures, governance, etc., with leading measures. How leaders go about undertaking this transformation is critical. It is not simply a case of saying, 'Stop using those measures'; that approach simply wouldn't work and would only make things worse. Instead, arbitrary measures need to be designed out and better replacement leading measures designed in. Understandably no one is going to give up their current measures unless there is a better alternative. However, it is safe to say there will be little or no change if current arbitrary measures aren't de-institutionalised.

Whilst we have pointed out that lagging measures are ineffective for managing a service organisation, for the foreseeable future lagging measures like profit and cost will continue to be a measure that boards, market analysts or ministers will continue to focus on. However, leaders can choose how to operationalise these measures. It is about learning to understand the relationship between leading and lagging measures. If leaders have different leading measures to guide their operations, and those measures help them understand how well they deliver to purpose, when those leading measures improve, that betterment translates into the betterment in lagging measures. Through the application of leading measures, leaders learn to understand the predictors of the lagging measures and gain confidence by paying attention to the leading, knowing that the lagging will follow.

Are you ready to focus on the road ahead and take your eyes off the rear-view mirror?

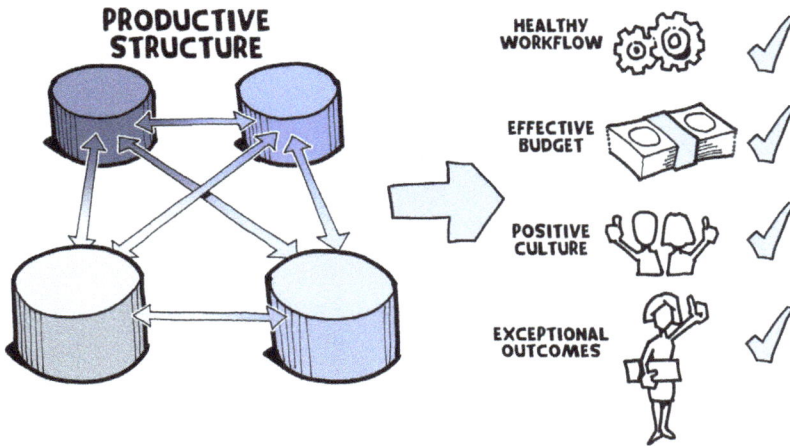

PRODUCTIVE STRUCTURE

HEALTHY WORKFLOW ✓

EFFECTIVE BUDGET ✓

POSITIVE CULTURE ✓

EXCEPTIONAL OUTCOMES ✓

17
DESIGNING PRODUCTIVE STRUCTURES

Organisational structures form the skeleton of an organisation. Productive structures support a healthy flow of work, effective use of budget, enable people to work productively, generate a positive culture, and create exceptional outcomes for customers. A well-designed organisation encourages qualities such as trust, fairness, openness, and mutual help. A poorly designed organisation encourages qualities such as coercion, use of power, secrecy, and self-interest, all of which inhibit communication, innovation, and collaboration.

Whilst hierarchies have acquired a poor reputation, we are not going to add to the calls for flatter structures. We know of no organisation that can run without both authority and some form of hierarchy, no matter how flat. We suggest that hierarchical structures are quite appropriate *if* they are based on organising complexity and dispersing authority.

The distribution of work through an organisation is a recognition that different people are capable of different work, even though very few organisations have a clearly defined concept of differing work complexity. Clearly, tasks of similar complexity can be bundled together to form a role that can be placed at an appropriate level in the organisation. This is what organisations attempt to do now, often in a muddled way because they do not have a clear means of differentiating between levels of management, capability, and complexity of tasks. Being clear about these concepts allows each level upwards to reflect a qualitatively more complex and abstract way to perceive and act in the world of work. More importantly, it equates to a specific rationale for the generally vague term of adding value. In a productive structure, each level has the potential to add value to the work of the level below by setting it in a broader, more complex context.

In nearly every organisation we encounter, organisations are unproductive due to poor design of their structure:

- roles are unclear

- authority and accountability are not clearly defined

- lateral role relationships are unclear

- there exist excess and compressed layers of management

- leaders are placed into roles based on tenure, experience, and/or personality

Whenever we encounter this, we ask leaders what theory they used to structure, or restructure, their organisation. Most answer that they based the structure on one or more of the following: gut feel, ensuring certain individuals kept their current status or role title, keeping people happy, ensuring that managers had a minimum or set amount of people reporting to them, or that a consultancy advised them. Although each technically uses theory, it is implicit theory, which is untestable and therefore more difficult to replicate or scale successfully. This presents an enormous risk and invariably leads to the creation of an 'unorganised' organisation with unclear objectives, the arbitrary use of power, excessive levels of activity and effort (much of it unproductive), a lack of clarity around people's roles, and poorly designed organisational systems and structures that hinder turning intention into reality. Invariably, further restructures result, each of which does little better than its predecessor.

Sound organisational theory is required to guide the creation of a productive structure. In our experience, the Stratified Systems Theory[70] of organisation has proven to be a particularly useful guide. The following real-life case study demonstrates how.

In a service organisation, the problem the executive leadership wanted to solve was to improve how people worked together and increase employee engagement. When we met with the executive leaders, they explained that the organisation had tried multiple approaches to solve these problems. The organisation had been through several restructures; replaced leaders who were deemed ineffective; put people through multiple training courses, surveys, profilers, psychometric assessments, and personality tests; had held team-building workshops and away days; run a 'working better together' program; utilised communication and change strategies to 'bring people along the journey'; and employed a CX team to improve employee experience; yet none of these approaches had improved how well people worked together or increased employee engagement. The executive leadership were frustrated and just wanted people to 'get along'.

---

70 Jaques, E., *Requisite Organization: A Total System for Effective Managerial Organization and Managerial Leadership for the 21st Century* (2nd ed.), Routledge, 2006.

The structure was typical of those in many service organisations. Roles were structured over six hierarchical levels:

ROLE	RESPONSIBILITY
CHIEF EXECUTIVE OFFICER	Delivering the strategy as defined by the board.
EXECUTIVE	Integrating the strategy as defined by the CEO within a division (Customer delivery, Finance and Risk, HR, Technology, etc.).
DEPARTMENT HEADS	Operationalising the strategy as defined by the Executive.
SENIOR LEADERS	Ensuring team leaders and team members comply with KPIs and standard processes as defined by the Executive and Department Heads. Managing backlogs.
TEAM LEADERS	Ensuring team members comply with KPIs and standard processes and work on backlogs.
TEAM MEMBERS	Meeting KPIs and complying with standard processes.

Table 1: Existing structure

Middle management's view was that 'everything was awesome'. However, after we interviewed a cross-section of employees, it became clear that, below the surface, there was dissatisfaction. Power, coercion, and self-interest were rife. Leaders were not held to account, and there were no consequences for their actions. There was a culture of busyness and surveillance. The structure was muddled. There was confusion around who did what. Subsequently, customer service, work efficiency, employee engagement, and operational costs were negatively affected.

We completed an organisational diagnostic, starting with a desktop structural review. This was a paper-based exercise that required the executive leaders, together with advice from us, to consider whether the current structural arrangements were appropriate, and what would need to change to better achieve the organisational purpose and goals. An analysis was made of the following critical issues:

- What is the work to be done that creates value?

- How should the required work be structured?

- How should the gap between what is required and what exists be addressed?

- What if there is not sufficient clarity of role relationships and appropriate authority?

- What is the best way to understand the use of power and assess where it is being applied?

The executive leadership worked through each of these critical issues, developing a shared understanding of what a productive structure would look like. The first step in this process was to understand both the primary and highest levels of complexity needed within the context of the organisation's purpose.

The first level of complexity was the front-line of the organisation, where services were delivered to a customer. Some work was transactional in nature, while other work was longer term and required the team member to think in terms of a time span of somewhere between one day and three months. The nature of this work was termed '**responding** to customers'.

Moving to the highest level of complexity: the organisation's board required someone to work on delivering the board's strategy whilst also managing a diverse group of external strategic stakeholders. This work was complex and required someone to work with a much broader time span – more than five years. The Chief Executive Officer undertook this work. The nature of this work was termed '**shaping** the organisation to deliver the strategy as defined by the board'.

The final step was to determine the intervening levels of complexity and the nature of the work required at each level. This work provided the framework for the executive leadership to see that to become more positively viewed and productive, the organisation needed to be structured to recognise the differing nature of work and complexity at each level (shaping, integrating, designing, optimising, and responding).

ROLE	NATURE OF WORK	COMPLEXITY (TIME SPAN)
CHIEF EXECUTIVE OFFICER	**Shaping** the organisation to deliver the strategy as defined by the board	Five to ten years
EXECUTIVE	**Integrating** the systems within a specific division to operationalise the strategy as defined by CEO	Two to five years
DEPARTMENT HEAD	**Designing** systems within a divisional context	One to two years
MANAGER	**Optimising** the work completed by team members	Three months to one year
TEAM MEMBER	**Responding** to customers	One day to three months

Table 2: Requisite structure

Table 2 represents the requisite structure for the organisation. Now that the executives understood how to structure the required work, they compared the current structure (table 1) with the requisite structure (table 2). A critical issue became visible – the current structure had too many layers.

Predictably, having too many layers in an organisation results in crowding of a level, or levels, in a structure. 'Crowding' is basically when too many people, usually managers, are asked to complete work of similar complexity. It leads to a lack of clarity and confusion around who the real boss is. In our experience, crowding is very common.

The crowding situation exposed the organisation to uses of power, and often led to dissatisfaction within the workforce. The executive leadership could now see some of the reasons why people did not work well together and why they had low employee engagement. And, as importantly, why previous attempts to solve these issues had not addressed the root cause. Subsequently, to address the gap between what was required and what currently existed, work began to put in place a structure that 'decongested' the levels through a process of understanding and creating role clarity.

EACH LAYER IN A STRUCTURE NEEDS TO WORK AT A DIFFERENT LEVEL OF COMPLEXITY AND ADD VALUE TO THE LAYER BELOW

There are two important principles for creating a requisite structure: at each level, people are required to work at a different level of complexity and capability; and each level needs to add value to the next level below. These two organising principles were vital for the executive to define the roles in the levels between the CEO and team members in their requisite structure, because the people in these roles invariably:

- have people reporting to them and they would have managerial accountability

- have a different level of authority than the people in roles below them

- ask other people to complete work

- give recognition for that work

- are accountable for the work of others

In this organisation, if people working in the levels between the CEO and team members could not add value to the people in the roles below, respect for their role was difficult to achieve. They were often viewed with suspicion and sometimes cynicism as to why their leader job existed at all.

Previously, the organisation had created a senior leader level in response to perceived people issues and span of control[71] problems.

---

71 Span of control, also known as management ratio, refers to the number of direct reports a manager has.

The senior leader level had been inserted above the team leaders and below the departmental heads. They were described as people leaders, meaning they were accountable for the performance of the team leaders and had the authority to assign them work to do.

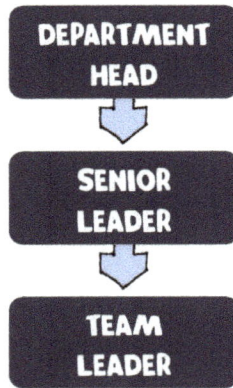

```
┌─────────────┐
│ DEPARTMENT  │
│    HEAD     │
└─────────────┘
      ⇩
┌─────────────┐
│   SENIOR    │
│   LEADER    │
└─────────────┘
      ⇩
┌─────────────┐
│    TEAM     │
│   LEADER    │
└─────────────┘
```

The response to this restructure was negative, because there was no noticeable difference between the team leader's work and the new senior leader's work. In other words, both roles had work with the same complexity. Worse still, the team leaders assumed they had done something wrong and felt like they were being surveilled by the senior leaders. We were asked to help the executive leaders to understand why this well-intended structure change had created such a negative outcome.

After interviewing all the leaders involved, it became apparent that the new senior leader layer of management had been put in place to act as surveillance to ensure compliance to multiple KPIs and standard processes. This compliance surveillance was of no value to either the team members or team leaders.

Predictably the senior leaders were rejected by everybody below them because they were perceived as not doing different work and could not add value to the level below. In response to the rejection, and following encouragement from department heads, the senior leaders predictably doubled down on their surveillance.

Coercive leadership was encouraged. For example, people were tasked to meet their numbers faster, or to work harder.

Chaos ensued, and the relationship between the team leaders and the senior leaders collapsed. Basically, these outcomes were caused by the failure to adhere to the two organising principles described previously – each layer needs to work at a different level of complexity and add value to the layer below it.

Once the critical issue of crowding and its causes had been revealed, the executive leaders began the work to create a requisite structure. The department heads were tasked to become plumbers – in other words, redesign and decongest the structure. Our guidance was to have only one manager accountable for other people within the same level, thus avoiding crowding by ensuring that each level added value to the level below. The department heads removed the senior leader layer, freeing the team leaders from the additional surveillance and coercive tactics. Critically, they provided role clarity, so the team leaders had the authority to lead their teams productively and could exercise their judgement and discretion when leading their teams.

IT IS BETTER TO BUILD RELATIONSHIPS BASED ON AUTHORITY RATHER THAN POWER

As we previously mentioned, in this organisation, power, coercion, and self-interest were rife. Although leaders had managerial accountability, it was common that there were no consequences for their actions. People tended to be overly managed and poorly led. There was confusion around who did what. There was little clarity on role relationships and appropriate authorities. Subsequently, customer service, work efficiency, employee engagement, and operational expenses were negatively affected. This was a critical issue that needed to be addressed.

However, before we explore the process for resolving these issues, we need to first clarify a key term we have introduced here – the term *managerial accountability*.

Consider the components of this term in turn. The word 'manager' is possibly one of the least understood terms in organisations. The definition we use for a manager is:

☑ A person who is accountable for their work and the work performance of others, such as a team.

Therefore, based on this clear definition, all people with someone reporting to them are managers. Does that mean every manager is a leader, as some people state, or is leadership superior to management? Managers are leaders because every manager is accountable for the leadership they provide to those who work for them. Within an employment hierarchy, all managers are leaders, but not all leaders are managers.

As for the term 'accountability', we define this as:

☑ An environment in which an individual can be called to account for their actions by another individual or body authorised by both parties.

The critical part of this statement is 'authorised by both parties'. Authority, in this context, is:

☑ The application of action in the context of the mutual acceptance of agreed limits.

Understanding the importance of authority as part of accountability is a critical element to developing role clarity. Without this understanding, leaders risk holding someone to account for something they don't have the authority to impact. We helped the executives see that this exact situation repeatedly occurred in their service organisation. For example, contact centre consultants were accountable for resolving customer issues, when in reality, the issues could only be fixed elsewhere in the organisation; operational leaders were held accountable for project delivery which relied on all the work being completed by IT; team leaders were asked to increase productivity, but other people could hand their teams work; the same team leaders were asked to improve processes, but weren't allowed to change anything unless the executive leaders approved it; CX teams designed processes but were never accountable for the outcome – the list went on and on. The executives learned it was quite common for people in roles to have all the accountability but none of the authority.

At the more senior levels, because authority associated with each role was not clearly defined and agreed, people were predictably overstepping their authority. A person making decisions beyond the limits of their authority is how we define power. Power emerged in this organisation because it was seen as the only way to get things done. The use of power was either inadvertent or deliberate, depending on the person or situation. In both cases, though, it led to relationships within the organisation being built on poor foundations and resulted in poor operational outcomes. Once this was understood, it was easy for the executive leadership to see why people were not just getting along.

As we have described, being a manager means being accountable for one's work and the work of others. Therefore, managerial accountability means a manager should be held to account for that work. Importantly, for a manager to have the best chance of being successful, they also need a clear articulation of their role authority. Without this, it is unfair to give recognition of how well or not a manager performs in their role.

In this organisation, the authority held by the various managerial levels was certainly not clear, and the significance of not having clarity was misunderstood. We found that this was most acutely evident at the team leader level. The team leader was the first level of manager in the organisation, but they also had the least amount of authority. They were held accountable for the performance of people, yet lacked the authority to influence those people. This was a fundamental structural flaw, one that is very common in service organisations.

It is a far more productive working environment if each person understands where each other's authority starts and finishes. There is also a minimum level of authority that any person who is responsible for the work of others requires, including first-level managers. That includes the ability to:

1. Veto the appointment of people to their team

2. Assign work to their team

3. Recognise and reward good performance

4. Initiate removal of people from their team

In this organisation, we asked each leader if they had this requisite minimum level of authority. The answer, predictably, was no. Without this authority, any leader, regardless of level, was being unfairly held to account and assessed. This lack of clarity created the environment for power to be used by someone either inadvertently or deliberately overstepping their level of role authority, because without a clear understanding of authority, using power had become the only way to get things done. Power structures had developed because accountability and authority were not clearly defined and mutually agreed upon as part of a role clarity process. This was one of the biggest issues affecting the organisation and the reason why many relationships between managers and team members were negatively viewed.

In addition to creating a productive structure, for this organisation role clarity was one of the most important elements of their leadership work. Once completed, it resolved a significant proportion of the perceived people issues that had emerged in the workplace.

REFLECTIONS

The case study we have described here is common. We believe it is also at the heart of the 'frozen middle', a term widely used to describe the problems associated with work within the middle management layer of an organisation.

As in the many previous attempts by this organisation, addressing the frozen middle problem is often undertaken without theory. Solutions typically lead to the removal of people and roles and the placement of people into a new structure based on tenure, experience, and personality, not on capability and complexity. There is no work done to understand if there is sufficient clarity of role relationships and appropriate authority. Predictably, the same issues continue to occur, despite the fact that people and roles have been changed.

The executives in the case study learned that it is far better to use sound theory to create a requisite structure that matches capability to complexity and to create clarity on role accountability and authority.

By unpicking the previous structure and its lack of clarity between levels of management, the complexity of tasks, and capability required, and through creating role clarity, the organisation obtained many quantifiable benefits:

- Excess managerial layers were removed, along with associated costs

- People at all levels gained a clearer understanding of what was expected of them

- People were enabled to use their full capabilities in exercising judgement and discretion in roles that enabled them to work productively to their potential

- Managers at all levels were able, and seen, to add value to their team members

- Excess monitoring, reporting, and other such unproductive activity were designed out

- Use of power, secrecy, and self-interest were removed

18
A CURE FOR THAT DÉJÀ VU FEELING OF CULTURAL RESISTANCE

A quick online search reveals lots of articles that describe cultural resistance as being one of the main barriers to successful change and transformation. For example, in 2021, *Harvard Business Review* reported: 'Change resistant managers anticipate that their C-suite leadership will largely revert to the behaviors they demonstrated before the pandemic… Almost a third of the people closest to the C-suite are either Change Resistant or Disaffected – and the same is true for about one-fourth of middle management … What CEOs and their teams have to recognize is that the executives working under them cannot be relied upon to fall into line and embrace calls for change based on new and urgent priorities.'[72]

Is the concept of cultural resistance thwarting organisational change new, or is it simply a case of déjà vu?

Back in 1980, Peter Keen wrote in his paper 'Information Systems and Organisational Change': 'Many writers on implementation stress the homeostatic behaviour of organizations and the need to "unfreeze the status quo." ... We now have adequate theories of implementation. We have less understanding of counterimplementation ... overt moves, often made by skilled actors, to prevent a disruption of the status quo.'[73]

It is worth noting here that Peter Keen has been ranked as one of the world's top 100 thought leaders in business and is one of the most cited researchers in academic and business literature. Yet, the problems he highlighted over 40 years ago still exist, and today are reported as revelatory news. It is almost as though we have learnt nothing from our experience!

Some leaders attempting to introduce change into their organisations, such as digital transformation or new ways of working, recognise the risk of concerted resistance from within. They attempt to address this resistance by shifting mindsets and culture through cultural change programs that involve things like defining corporate values and behaviours, communication strategies, and training. Although born from reasonable-sounding ideas, these solutions inevitably fall short. They disappear without trace or, worse, are replaced by increased cynicism about any benefits accruing from innovation and change.

Good theory is an essential prerequisite for culture change to be successful and to overcome any cultural resistance. It guides the change, with a clear understanding and definition of culture and the practical methods and leadership tools to change culture.

---

72 'Are Your Managers in Sync with Your Change Strategy?', Joseph Fuller and Bill Theofilou, *Harvard Business Review*, 4 Mar 2021.

73 'Information Systems and Organizational Change', Peter G. W. Keen, Center for Information Systems Research, Alfred P. Sloan School of Management, Massachusetts Institute of Technology, Cambridge, MA, May 1980, pp. 6–11.

In this chapter, we explore the theory behind social cohesion, human behaviour, and values. We also clearly define what creates culture. These sections form the context to examine how to successfully achieve culture change and overcome cultural resistance.

HUMAN BEHAVIOUR AND VALUES

Fundamentally, for any organisational change to be successful, a change in people's behaviour is required.

There is a set of principles that underpins people's behaviour and the subsequent social groups they form. This section expands on four of those principles:

Principle 1: People need to be able to predict their environments

Principle 2: People do not like to be objectified

Principle 3: People's behaviour is based on universal values

Principle 4: People form cultures based on mythologies

Understanding each of these principles is essential before exploring whether cultural change is possible.

PRINCIPLE 1: PEOPLE NEED TO BE ABLE TO PREDICT THEIR ENVIRONMENTS

The majority of time, people do not think about their environment. People only tend to become aware of their environment when their expectations or predictions are challenged. For example, when a friend, work colleague, or family member behaves differently to what is expected, people want to understand why. In circumstances such as these, if people cannot come up with an explanation, they will probably invent one, so they can rationalise the change in behaviour.

It is human nature to not feel safe in any environment unless we can predict what will happen next. The process of surveying our environment and creating our very own way of predicting and classifying others' behaviour starts the moment we are born. People continue this classification process all their lives. At work, people's environment is determined by factors such as who they sit next to, who their manager is, what tasks they are given to do, what new projects are starting, and so on. People find it very difficult to concentrate or be productive if they must constantly try to make sense of and adapt to a changing environment.

The impacts of unpredictable environments on organisations can be quite damaging. We are aware of one organisation where there had been so many restructures that employees were just biding their time until the next one. Consequently, people only made short-term decisions, knowing that there was little point in thinking long term, as the structure would predictably change again, soon.

For effective change, leaders need to recognise that successful change relies on people feeling safe that they can predict their environment, both in terms of how others behave and how others react to them.

PRINCIPLE 2: PEOPLE DO NOT LIKE TO BE OBJECTIFIED

This common-sense statement – that people are not objects – is central to understanding change processes. Despite this, in our experience, it appears to be easily forgotten. (See People are not machines, page 14, in chapter 1.)

If a person was an object, we would not have to worry about will or intent. The object would react to any action on it in a consistent and predictable way. We would not have to consider what the object thinks. The object would not consider our intent as either positive or negative; nor would it have any notion of its own value, or the value we attribute to it. The reality is, though, that people are not objects. The distinction between people and objects may seem simple and obvious. However, despite this simplicity, we all muddle them up sometimes.

We hear about 'FTE reduction' and 'resource efficiency'. These phrases do not mention people; neither does the phrase 'cultural change'. Discussions within organisations can assume people have no will, or that their will is a nuisance. It can be comforting for some leaders to assume people's behaviour will change based on rational argument, and as a result, they expect people to comply based purely on objective logic. However, this thinking is flawed – it gives the illusion that people can be controlled, which, unsurprisingly, leads to poor organisational outcomes. While objects can be controlled, people cannot. People can only be influenced. Leaders might lament, 'Why don't they get it?' However, treating people as objects is likely, at a minimum, to result in cynicism and possibly malicious (and temporary) compliance.

Any discussion of organisational change needs to address how behaviour is influenced. People will not act as objects and merely do as they are instructed. In some cases, people will feel threatened by context changes, knowing they may run the risk of being classified as change resistant if they speak up. If their context is constantly changing, and they feel that this is not fair and impacts their performance, or they feel admonished if they speak up, they may conclude that their manager does not care how they view or experience the situation they find themselves in. In short, people may feel that they are being objectified: being treated as an object, an employee number, or a cog in the machine.

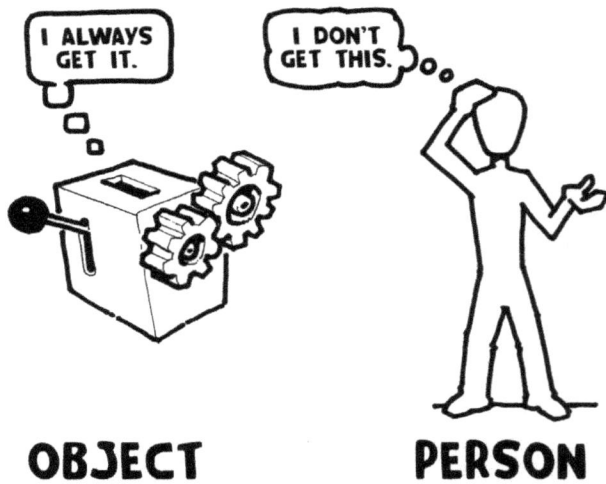

OBJECT **PERSON**

A case in point is a cultural change program where the idea was to train leaders in how to be what was termed 'servant leaders'. The new thinking was that leaders were employed to serve their team members, instead of the traditional focus of serving the boss. In a two-day training course, leaders were given a badge stating 'I'm here to serve' to wear back in the office. The leaders completed the training and, upon returning to their desks, threw the badge in a drawer. Despite feeling dehumanised, they never voiced their concerns during the training, as they were worried about the implications of speaking up and being labelled as change resistant.

If we are disciplined about treating people as more than just objects, we can start to understand how people view the world. We need to understand not only what the organisation needs but also what people need, and what they assess as worthy and unworthy. This is a fundamental component for truly effective culture change.

PRINCIPLE 3: PEOPLE'S BEHAVIOUR IS BASED ON UNIVERSAL VALUES

The third principle is that all people, societies, and organisations share the same set of universal values. Before you go 'Hang on', because you can immediately think of organisations and people who don't appear to hold the same set of values as you, hold that thought until you have had a chance to reflect on the following discussion.

Human behaviour is based on a universal set of six values. These six values are essential components of constructive social relationships that result in productive social cohesion. Each value describes a behaviour: loving, trustworthy, respectful, courageous, honest, and fair. Why these six values? Because these are the values that have stood up to thorough testing in private, public, and voluntary organisations, and in a wide variety of communities and countries around the world.[74]

Values cannot be seen, but they can be observed through what other people say and how they behave. Like many, we have heard the expression 'They have different values to us', a phrase that is often used to explain a behaviour observed in others, and usually a behaviour judged as negative by the observer. It is an example of the 'us vs. them' thinking: 'It's not us, it's them!' But how can this be, if people share the same universal values? So, whilst it is true that behaviours may differ, the universal values by which they are assessed do not differ.

Consider each of these universal values as a continuum from positive to negative (see figure 1, below). Behaviour at the positive

---

74 See Macdonald, Burke and Stewart, *Systems leadership: Creating Positive Organisations*, 2nd edition, which provides more detail and examples of worldwide research.

end of the continuum strengthens a social group; behaviour at the negative end weakens and eventually destroys a social group.

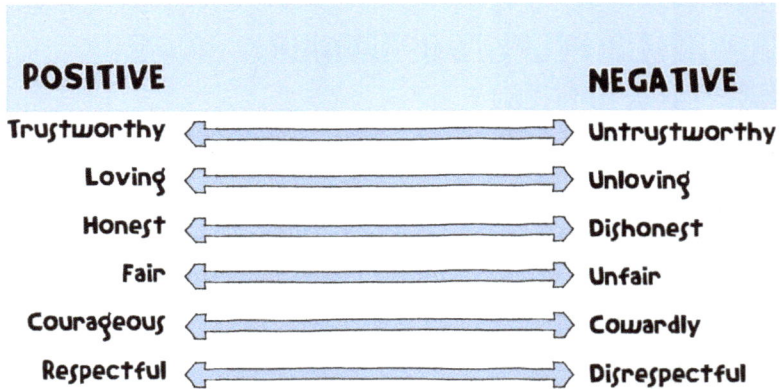

POSITIVE   **NEGATIVE**

Trustworthy ⟸————————⟹ Untrustworthy

Loving ⟸————————⟹ Unloving

Honest ⟸————————⟹ Dishonest

Fair ⟸————————⟹ Unfair

Courageous ⟸————————⟹ Cowardly

Respectful ⟸————————⟹ Disrespectful

Figure 1: Values continua

Universal values are not a matter of choice, which is why organisational values fail as a method to promote culture change. We cannot pick and/or choose values. We also cannot say, 'I will adopt these universal values as the new corporate values'. You are already being judged against them, whether you adopt them or not!

PRINCIPLE 4: PEOPLE FORM CULTURES BASED ON MYTHOLOGIES

The final principle to examine before we explore changing cultures is how cultures are formed.

The starting point for this is to define what is culture. The definition that we have found useful when discussing culture in an organisational setting is:

☑   A culture is a group of people who share a common set of mythologies.

That is, they share assumptions and beliefs about behaviours demonstrating values positively and negatively. Essentially, the more mythologies people have in common, the stronger the culture.

In other words, people are drawn to other people who agree with what they think constitutes positive or negative behaviour. They use shared universal values to explain and put value to the observed behaviour. Generally, this interpretation of behaviour is gained through a story or mythology. In this context, the precise definition of mythology is:

The underlying assumption and current belief as to what is positively valued behaviour and what behaviour is negatively valued, and why it is so.

Mythologies are a mixture of mythos (stories with emotional content) and logos (rationality).

In a practical sense, we all view our world through a mythological lens. This lens is unique to us and has been formed over time through exposure to the stories expressed by our family, friends, and work colleagues, or through education, media, and films. This is our worldview, and it is built through our own experience and observation. Basically, we observe behaviour, process it through our lens, and make a judgement as to where that behaviour sits on the values continua described in the previous section (see figure 1, above).

People tend to create social bonds with people who agree with their interpretation of behaviour, and this becomes the basis of a culture. The strength of a culture is dependent on the extent that people share a mythology, the importance of the mythologies to the people concerned, and the significance of the observed behaviour.

Whilst viewing culture in this way can be liberating, it also illustrates how complex cultures can be. If culture is unique to an individual, then within an organisation there will be multiple cultures. Furthermore, cultures are formed from people classifying every interaction with another person. Imagine how many interactions people have on a daily, weekly, or monthly basis. That is what makes culture both complex and fascinating, and brings into sharp focus the fundamental reason why culture cannot be changed through approaches such as sitting in a meeting room with a consultant or by a change communication team using training materials, screensavers, and posters.

It is also the reason why leaders who try to introduce a monoculture across the organisation inevitably fail.[75] A monoculture is typically articulated, communicated, and implemented through corporate values that are a representation of the specific worldview

---

75 By monoculture, we mean a single, homogeneous culture, without diversity or dissension.

of the people who developed them. They are typically built in the boardroom, based on organisational vision or mission statements. They contain words such as honesty, innovation, integrity, and togetherness, to name but a few. While these are all laudable, writing them on a wall does not create a culture. A monoculture approach also suggests that we maintain a set of values at work that are different from the ones we maintain elsewhere. In other words, as soon as we walk through the office doors, we are expected to change our values and, therefore, behaviour. At best, that is incongruent; at worst, that is like suggesting we must become someone completely different to fit in at work.

Forming culture must be embraced as an emergent process. Culture is something that can be understood but cannot be fixed at any one point in time or changed through rational explanation or coercion. Remember, we are talking about human behaviour and its inherent complexities.

We contend that we share universal human values which are immutable, and that we hold those values regardless of where we are or what we are doing. This, in turn, implies that monocultures are inappropriate and organisational values are irrelevant. If corporate values include trust or fairness, but exclude courage or love, the leader's behaviour will still be judged against all six universal values – they will still be judged on how courageous, compassionate, and caring they are anyway.

The question is how these principles that underpin human behaviour can be applied as a practical method to change culture within organisations.

UNDERSTANDING EXISTING ORGANISATIONAL CULTURE

As we have discussed, effective culture change requires acknowledging that multiple cultures are likely to exist in an organisation and, thus, any approach that requires a monoculture at its core will ultimately fail. Instead, the first step in culture change is to understand the extent to which current culture is shared across the organisation and how the existing organisational culture differs from the desired culture.

As mythologies change over time, understanding the current organisational culture needs to be done continuously and systematically. This involves understanding how employees experience their work, their leaders, their colleagues, and the organisation.

EXISTING CULTURE

Described in terms of people's mythologies about themselves, the organisation and their leader

Rather than the done-to-death pulse surveys every six months or annual employee engagement surveys, a significantly more informative and practical method to achieve this is to interview, one on one, a cross-section of employees. Questions centre on each person's experience of working in the organisation, and focus on: *What am I meant to be doing? How am I doing? What is my future? What is it like to work together?*

Once the interviews conclude, statements can be analysed, and those that are common can be interpreted to formulate a current set of mythologies. As leadership behaviour is highly symbolic, these interviews often reveal insights about negatively or positively perceived leadership behaviours. This data is useful for leaders to understand the effectiveness of current leadership and to understand the gaps (if any) between the current and desired organisational culture. This unique approach gives leaders an understanding of current mythologies, to what extent are they shared, and whether they are negative or positive in nature.

CHANGING CULTURE AND OVERCOMING RESISTANCE

A desired organisational culture is described in terms of how leaders would like people to behave and how they would like people to view their work, their leader, and the organisation. If the current organisational culture is different to the one that is desired, the culture needs to change.

DESIRED CULTURE

Described in terms of
how you would
like people to behave,
to view their work
and their leader

We know that successful culture change requires a change in people's behaviour, and in the previous sections of this chapter we have discussed the theory and principles that underpin people's behaviour. The purpose of leadership is to find effective ways to engender these behavioural changes by using good theory, but in such a way that it does not lead to cultural resistance.

There is also a common assumption that people are resistant to change, and that this resistance is inherent. In fact, we have found people are remarkably interested in change. From an early age, we experiment, try new approaches, learn, and test. The problem isn't so much that people are resistant to change; it is that they are resistant to the way in which change is being effected. So, what needs to happen instead, if behavioural change and, thus, culture change are to be successful?

First, we know no amount of rational debate or coercion will change someone's worldview. The only process that will change a person's worldview is through *dissonance*, a challenge, major or minor, to someone's worldview. As a simple illustration, consider the fact that there are a group of people, including some scientists, who believe the earth is flat. No amount of rational debate, argument, or videos taken from rockets convinces them otherwise. However, put them in a rocket and allow them to see the earth as a globe for themselves and imagine the dissonance these people would experience. Without dissonance, people's expectations and predictions will always be deemed, in their minds, as correct, based on their current perspective – they will resist, thinking: *Why should I change?*

In addition to experiencing dissonance, a person will only change their behaviour if they sense that change will be of benefit to them, the organisation, and customers, and that they are part of the change. In other words, they are not objectified, and change is not rolled out or 'done' to them. This is one of the principles we discussed earlier.

Thus, enabling change in people's behaviour creates the way forward to effectively introduce culture change. Leaders can work to change and sustain the culture that they desire by using three leadership tools: leadership behaviour (what we do and say), organisational system design (how we do things), and symbols (non-verbal messages of what we do and how we do it). Importantly, these leadership tools need to be used consistently and persistently, with coherence and without contradiction. Failure to do this inevitably creates cynicism, distrust, and negative mythologies, the very outcomes that leaders do not want.

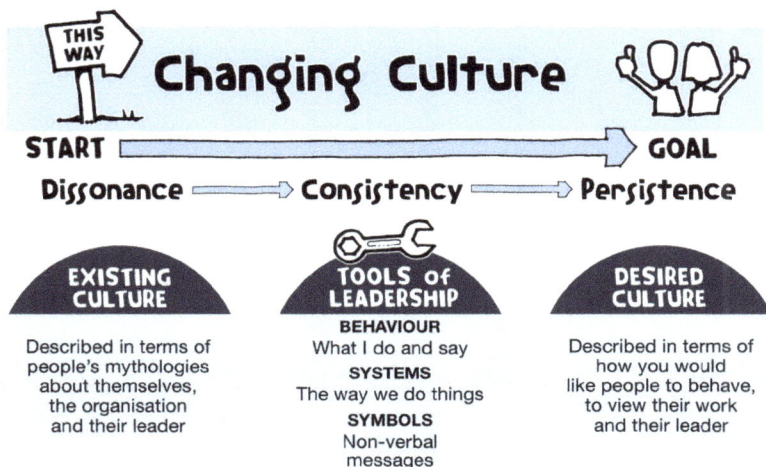

THIS WAY **Changing Culture**

START ⟹ **GOAL**

Dissonance ⟹ **Consistency** ⟹ **Persistence**

EXISTING CULTURE	TOOLS of LEADERSHIP	DESIRED CULTURE
Described in terms of people's mythologies about themselves, the organisation and their leader	**BEHAVIOUR** What I do and say **SYSTEMS** The way we do things **SYMBOLS** Non-verbal messages	Described in terms of how you would like people to behave, to view their work and their leader

If, as progressive leaders, you commit to understanding current mythologies, coherently using the tools of leadership, and doing so consistently and with persistence, you will be able to create a productive culture. Positive behaviour abounds, and resistance is no longer prevalent.

Let's consign cultural resistance to the past, and stop experiencing more déjà vu!

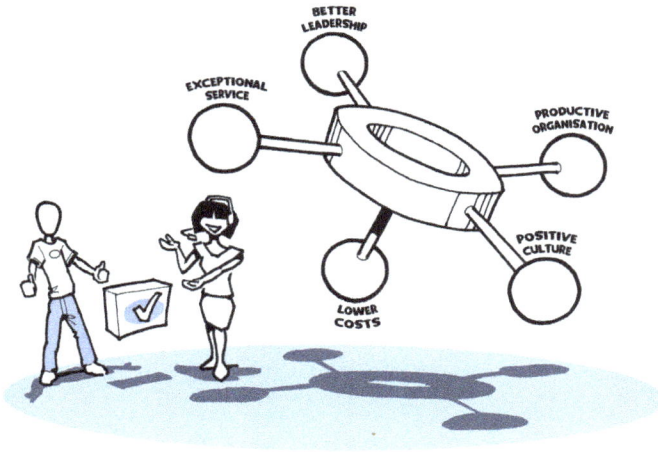

CASE STUDIES WITH REAL TANGIBLE RESULTS

Many books have been written about how to improve service, leadership, and culture, but very few attempt to link theory and ideas with actual, specific outcomes. Some may make general claims of a significant increase in productivity or efficiency, but do not provide supporting data.

We believe it is important to provide this data, so, in addition to the examples and case studies provided in previous articles and chapters, we have included several case studies here that describe in concrete terms the astonishing results achieved when progressive leaders have reconceived service delivery, leadership, and culture to create more positively viewed and productive service organisations.

CASE STUDY 1: INSURANCE CLAIMS

CONSUMER SATISFIED ✓ INSURER SATISFIED ✓ REGULATOR SATISFIED ✓

Imagine if you had to claim on your personal insurance. It could be that you have been injured and are unable to work and therefore need to claim for loss of income. It could be that you have had a serious illness, which has made it difficult or impossible for you to work, and you need financial help in the form of a trauma payment or total and permanent disability cover. It could be that you have been diagnosed with a terminal illness, or that someone in your family has died. I think you would agree, each instance is an extremely challenging life event. It is also why many people take out insurance policies. It gives peace of mind that, should the unthinkable happen, they will have support for themselves and their families at times of significant financial and emotional stress.

MAKING AN INSURANCE CLAIM SHOULD BE STRESS FREE

When people are dealing with challenging life circumstances, and at a point when they may feel vulnerable, making an insurance claim should be simple, stress-free, and lead to an outcome in days, not months. The Australian Securities and Investments Commission (ASIC) states that: 'For consumers, the intrinsic value of an insurance product is in the ability to make a successful claim when an insured event occurs'.[76] We agree. Many people chase the lowest insurance premiums; however, the only time you know whether your insurance policy and company is any good is when you make a claim.

---

76 Report 498, 'Life insurance claims: An industry review', Australian Securities and Investments Commission (ASIC), Oct 2016.

There is agreement amongst the regulators that the consumer experience during the claims process must be improved. Various reports and codes have highlighted the areas that need improvement, such as the experience at the time of claim, removing the complexity and confusing nature of the claims process, and addressing the unacceptable time period a claim can take to be settled.

In Australia, since 2019, the Australian Prudential Regulation Authority (APRA) and the Australian Securities and Investments Commission (ASIC) have released a series of publications and an online tool allowing policyholders – for the first time – to compare life insurers' performance in handling claims and disputes.[77] This information includes claims handling timeframes and dispute levels across all policy types[78] aimed at making it easier to compare life insurers' performance in handling claims and disputes.[79]

Speaking at the Australian Financial Services Council Life Insurance Summit, Emma Curtis, ASIC Senior Executive Leader – Insurers, Financial Services and Wealth group, said, 'What I would do is call on the industry to help us regulate you better collaboratively and ... help steer the industry towards consumer-centric outcomes'.[80]

---

77 APRA and ASIC publish world-leading life insurance data, press release, Australian Prudential Regulation Authority (APRA), 29 Mar 2019.

78 APRA sets expectations for improvements to claims handling, press release, Australian Prudential Regulation Authority (APRA), 12 Oct 2016.

79 APRA and ASIC publish latest data on life insurance claims and disputes, news release, Australian Prudential Regulation Authority (APRA), 20 Oct 2020.

80 'Industry needs to collaborate with regulators: ASIC', Chris Dastoor, MONEYIMANAGEMENT, 21 April 2021.

REDUCE COSTS AND IMPROVE SERVICE BY MAKING THE CONSUMER THE FOCAL POINT OF REFORM

Change must happen. That much is clear. The challenge for leaders is how to make changes that result in real improvement for consumers while reducing the cost of delivery and compliance.

In our experience, when we observe leaders using conventional approaches to improve their claims services and comply with new regulations, changes take too long to implement and often involve expensive investment in IT. Inevitably, technology project costs escalate, the time required to deliver increases, and, often, despite this extra expense and time, the results delivered fall well short of expectations or, worse, lock in inefficient operating models into 'IT concrete', making future changes even more difficult and expensive.

Sound organisational theory, practical methods, and leadership tools, are required to make changes that result in real improvement for consumers while ensuring the cost of delivery and compliance reduce.

In a particular financial services organisation, the executive leadership wanted to improve their claims service by allowing greater flexibility in how consumers could interact with their organisation, reduce decision and payment time frames, reduce costs, and meet new industry-standard regulations.

Over several years a number of change initiatives had been undertaken to achieve these goals; for example, educating consumers on the claims process and how to navigate it when they initiated a claim, implementing case management, hiring senior claims assessors, effecting several restructures, and implementing targets and service level agreements.

Despite hefty investment and long time scales, each of these initiatives failed to achieve the anticipated results. Instead of reduced decision and payment timeframes, both, in fact, increased. Costs also increased, instead of reducing. These issues were hindering the organisation's ability to meet the new regulation standards. As a result, claims leaders had requested additional resources, citing an increase in the number of claims being placed on the service as the cause of the increased timeframes. Additional staff were hired, but, once again, performance didn't improve.

In a further attempt to improve the claims service and reduce costs, the executive turned to technology. There was a technology-first philosophy firmly embedded in the organisation, and multimillion-dollar projects were undertaken. The first was to implement a digital workflow tool. Countless hours were spent mapping the current claims processes and digitising them. A plethora of triggers were implemented in the tool, which would route or divert claims to various specialists based on rules. A new claims performance dashboard was also created, which used the workflow data to generate reports on the types of claims received, claim durations, team members' productivity, adherence to targets and service level agreements, and costs.

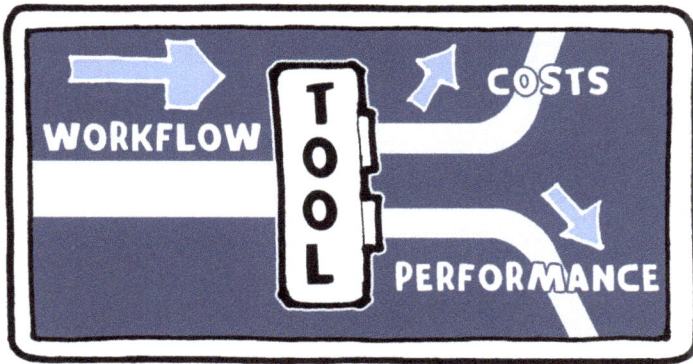

Unfortunately, after the implementation of the digital workflow tool and claims performance dashboard, performance continued to decline and costs increased. As is typical in many service organisations, the decision was made to invest in more technology to solve the problem, which further compounded the situation.

A progressive leader from the organisation contacted us for help. They could see an endless spend on technology wasn't proving to be the answer to their problems. We explained that, in our experience, applying technology to already ineffective work designs predictably leads to frustration, failure, and lament.

What needed to change first was the way in which the work was designed, organised, and managed. And, critically, that change should be consumer led, not technology led. We suggested that the consumer was put at the centre of any reform, and the consumer's perspective should be the focus for improving the insurance claims services.

We worked with leaders of the claims area to help them take a consumer's perspective and learn first-hand what was happening in their service. Through an experiential exercise, they learnt what creates value for consumers and how well the organisation's claims services were designed to deliver value. Studying a variety of different claim types, this new first-hand knowledge revealed:

- The typical and predictable consumer demands placed on the service, and how well their services were designed to deliver value for each of those demands

- The amount of unproductive activity (cost) inherent in the current organisational systems and structures and, more importantly, the causes of these costs

- The impact the organisational systems and structures had on productive behaviour and activity

- How people experienced their work, their leader, and the claims area

- Shared mythologies underpinning the existing culture

We asked the leaders to establish what mattered to consumers when it came to using the organisation's claims services. When talking to colleagues, the leaders found that there were a lot of assumptions about what consumers wanted. Customer experience (CX) experts and subject matter experts (SMEs) had held workshops to brainstorm what they thought were the consumers wants and needs. They also researched what other claims providers were doing. Together, this had formed the basis of what they assumed consumers needed. No one, though, had thought to engage with consumers directly to gain a true understanding of what creates value for them through learning their circumstances, needs, and issues.

We suggested that previous claimants be contacted, which revealed that what mattered to consumers was that they were eligible, the length of time it took for them to get a decision, that they got the right amount of money, what choice they had about when and how they received their payment, that they were able to deal with the same person, and that the organisation didn't cause them further stress and anxiety at their time of need. The leaders learned that the direct feedback from consumers conflicted with the previous CX and SME assumptions. For example, working to the CX and SME assumptions, consumers had previously been advised of service levels, not how long it would take for them to receive payment; they would deal with multiple people, not a single person; and every eligible claim was paid on the same date and in the same way, without variation.

It was also learned that consumers wanted to lodge claims in different ways. For example, a small cohort wanted to use a form, others wanted to do it online, and the biggest cohort wanted to do it over the phone. Again, these actual wants and needs conflicted with the previous assumptions. It had been assumed that *every* consumer would want to claim online, lodge documents online, and would want to see the progress of their claim online too. It became apparent that forcing consumers to transact online had frustrated a large percentage of people at their time of great need.

ORGANISATION   CONSUMERS

Next, the claims leaders looked at the number of claims received per week in a control chart. (See chapter 16, Are you running your organisation through the rear-view mirror?) There was a mythology in place that the number of claims received was on the increase; however, the control chart revealed that, in fact, the number of claims received per week had remained stable.

Looking at the claims performance dashboard reporting, it showed that claim durations were increasing but were still within agreed service level limits. Clearly, from a consumer's perspective, the claim would start when they first contacted the organisation, and end when they received a decision and their payment. But the claims leaders learned that within the claims team, the clock started only when all claim information was received from the consumer. It could take several weeks and lots of to and fro between the consumer and the claims team to receive all information. Consumers had to provide various proofs of identity, complete multiple forms, and provide supporting evidence, all of which, from a consumer's point of view, was part of the timeline, but not from the organisation's perspective. Once all initial claim information had been received, and the claim had been started, each time the consumer was asked for further information, the clock stopped until it was received, at which point the clock restarted. When asked why this was done, people in the claims team said that they were aware that the average time frame for a claim had increased and, therefore, they were focused on trying to make the numbers look better.

Via the claims performance dashboards, leaders could easily find out how much it cost to do a certain activity, how people were tracking against targets and service levels, and the status of each claim. However, when we asked them to find out how long claims took, end to end, from when a consumer first contacted the organisation until their claim was paid, they were unable to obtain that data. This data had to be extracted from various IT databases and placed into a control chart. It was a shock to the claims leaders when a true reflection of performance from a consumer's point of view – end-to-end resolution of the claim – was understood.

After learning the true duration for claims, we asked the leaders to follow claims through the various specialists involved in completing a claim. They found that working to service level agreements and targets, each of these specialists picked up a claim from their work queue, completed their portion of the work, then either passed it onto the next specialist or passed it back to the previous specialist if there was a discrepancy.

The leaders learned that:

- Consumers were asked for further information up to 20 times per claim

- Claims were handed to different specialists multiple times

- The same documentation was checked multiple times by different people

- Decisions were checked multiple times by different people

- There was a lack of clarity and agreement on the authority associated with each role

- Power structures had developed because managers would overstep their authority

- Claims team members and managers had become overly reliant on standard processes and complicated compliance regimes, had become overly risk averse, and had outsourced decisions to external parties such as Legal and Risk teams

- Over 90 per cent of the activity in the process did not directly contribute to settling the claim and was, therefore, unproductive activity

- Claims were diarised to service level agreement (SLA) timeframes and not worked on until the SLA was close to being breached

- Even a simple and straightforward claim would take months to complete

When observing the normal functioning of the claims work, some of the leaders asked colleagues whether they felt comfortable ignoring some of the red tape or not perform certain activities that, to them, obviously added no value. Each time their colleagues said they couldn't, because the policies, systems, processes, rules, or the design of IT tools didn't allow for that judgement or discretion. The executives quickly learned that no one, not team members, team leaders, or even claims managers, had the authority to change a system.

The leaders asked members of the claims teams what their managers paid attention to and were told that managers fixated on managing people's activity – how many things they did, how long it took them to do each task, what was in their queue, and so on. This had created a burgeoning and bureaucratic measurement system. Employees were regularly monitored and surveilled using technology to feed the measurement system.

Rather than starting with a purpose defined from the intent of the claims service ('Pay me what I'm entitled to'), a de facto purpose of make the numbers was evident. A singular focus on making the numbers capped performance, and drove unproductive behaviour and activity, because work was undertaken where the only intent was to make the bosses happy.

The claims managers paid attention to things that mattered to them – and what they paid attention to got done. The impact was that more people in the claims teams focused on making the numbers, instead of on achieving the purpose the claims service had been set up to accomplish. The following diagram illustrates how this relationship operated in practice.

MEASURES	Targets, incentives, work states, standards
⬇	
PURPOSE	Make the numbers
⬇	
WORK	Case manage; diarise & wait; follow the process; specialise & functionalise; stop the clock

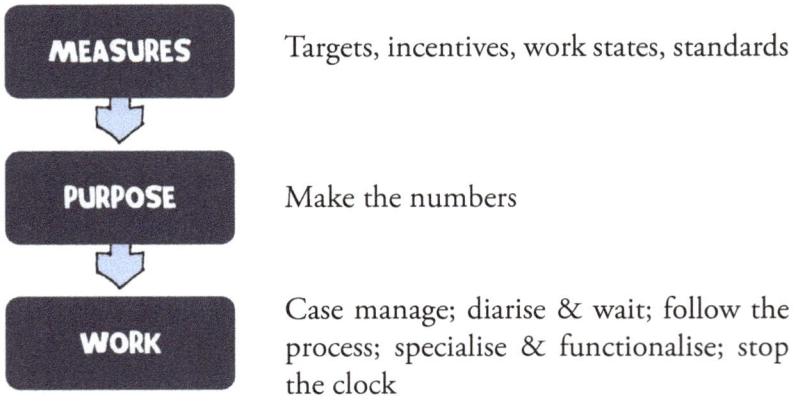

As a result of these experiential learning experiences, the claims leaders couldn't un-see what they had seen with their own eyes and un-hear what they had heard with their own ears. We asked the leaders to reflect on the following:

1. Why is it like this?

2. What is the effect on people claiming at a difficult time in their life?

3. How much is this costing the organisation?

The claims leaders had learnt that their current organisational systems and structures caused high levels of failure demand, lots of unproductive activity, increased backlogs of work, and unneeded operational expense. The learning process that had been undertaken from the consumer's perspective had diagnosed significant and previously hidden improvement opportunities in how to effectively service consumers at a time of great need, work more efficiently, better meet regulation, and reduce operating costs. Therefore, the decision was taken to redesign both the organisational systems and structures to improve the service.

**HIDDEN
IMPROVEMENT
OPPORTUNITIES**

We advised that the most effective approach, and certainly a less costly one than those taken to date, was to redesign the claims services using the following steps:

1. Determine what creates value for people claiming and how best to service them, and use that information to set the context for improvement

2. Organise and enable people to deliver outcomes more effectively, supported by productive organisational systems and structures

3. And, only then, apply the minimum required technology that complements the more effective organisational systems and structures, enhances cognitive processes, and automates simple and repetitive tasks

It was our experience that adopting this unique three-step approach would enable the organisation to achieve improved claim outcomes in months, not years. And in doing so, service to consumers would quickly improve, and, at the same time, delivery and compliance costs would plummet.

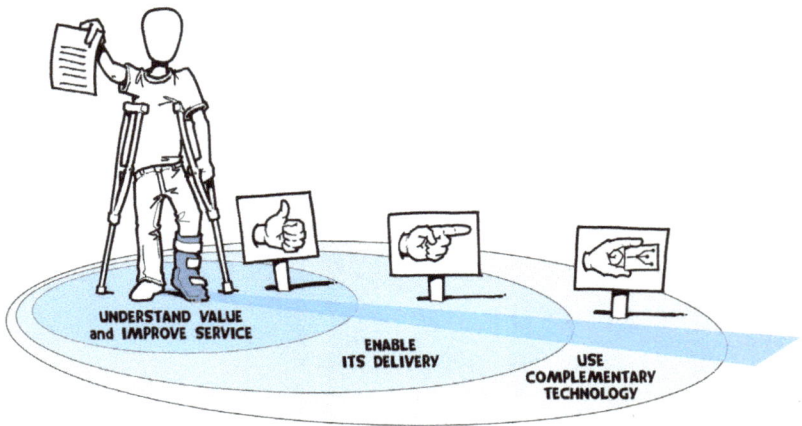

The real-life results were compelling. After applying this three-step approach, a productive structure was designed and implemented. (See chapter 17, Designing productive structures.) As a result, excess managerial layers were removed, people at all levels gained a clearer understanding of what was expected of them, people were enabled to use their full capabilities in exercising judgement and discretion in roles that freed them to work productively (see chapter 15, Turning intention into productive reality), and a far more productive working environment was created, so that each person understood where each other's authority started and finished. (See the section It is better to build relationships based on authority rather than power, in chapter 17, page 195.) Existing organisational systems were diagnosed, redesigned, and implemented. (See chapter 14, Liberating people and organisations from stultifying systems.) Leaders worked to change and sustain culture by using three leadership tools: leadership behaviour, organisational system design, and symbols (See chapter 18, A cure for that déjà vu feeling of cultural resistance.)

Rather than having separate functions to pass work between each other to process life insurance claims, teams with the required skill sets were formed. Each team had the capability and authority to use judgement and discretion to complete the minimum required work, for example, claim assessment. Technologists worked alongside their front-line colleagues taking new insurance claims to understand what creates value for consumers. This created a shared body of knowledge that related back to consumers and the way consumer work was done. The technologists were able to see first-hand that much of the organisation's IT tools were hindering their colleagues from creating value for consumers. Many of the business rules in the process were embedded in the tools, and forced people to follow the process, no matter how unproductive some of the steps were. With this knowledge, the technologists could understand and identify where technology could complement human activity, rather than control it. The IT leaders focused on creating the capability so that when a productive organisational system was designed and implemented, the technology could change and adapt with it. As a result:

- Their processing time for life insurance claims, from claim notification to decision, reduced by over 80 per cent

- Over 96 per cent of the previous steps for life insurance claims were removed, as they were revealed to be unproductive activities from a consumer's perspective

- Their processing time for medical insurance claims, from claim notification to decision, reduced by over 45 per cent

- Over 65 per cent of the previous steps for medical insurance claims were removed, as they were revealed to be unproductive activities from a consumer's perspective

- The spend on IT for meeting new regulations was less than a tenth of what had been originally budgeted

From a consumer's point of view, at a time when people are experiencing challenging life circumstances, and at a point when many feel vulnerable, a simple and straightforward service is of critical importance to them, and they have been vocal in their praise of the improved service.

Progressive leaders can make this example the new norm for the service industry, rather than the exception. After all, this three-step approach can be applied to any process-based service, including financial services, planning and development, repairs, social care, health, installations, allocations, and repairs and maintenance. Imagine! Satisfied customers and significant quantifiable savings in cost and processing times just waiting to be realised.

CASE STUDY 2: IT SERVICE MANAGEMENT

Most organisations rely on various IT services for their operations. If there is an unplanned interruption or degradation in function in IT services, it can hinder both the user's ability to do their work and customer's ability to get their demand met from a service.

To minimise disruption, organisations typically have a well-defined Incident Management process to restore IT services to their normal state as quickly as possible. Restoration may sometimes include implementing a workaround until a permanent solution is provided.

In one private sector organisation, they adopted and implemented industry best-practice frameworks and procedures for Incident Management and Problem Management. They also purchased the top-rated cloud-based service management software and digitised workflows. In the eventuality an incident interrupted normal operation in one or more IT services, these frameworks, processes, and digitised workflows would be enacted. Despite the significant financial investment in this service management software, and the considerable effort expended on documenting and digitising workflows and training staff in frameworks, incidents would often still take too long to resolve, or, in some cases, not be resolved at all.

We worked with the IT leadership to help them gain a customer's and user's perspective of service management as a prelude to improvement. Through an experiential exercise, they learned first-hand:

- The typical and predictable demands placed on service management, and how well their services were designed to deliver value for each of those demands

- The amount of unproductive activity (cost) inherent in the current organisational systems and structures, and, more importantly, the causes of these costs

- The impact the organisational systems and structures had on productive behaviour and activity

- How people experienced their work, their leader, and the IT department

- Shared mythologies underpinning existing culture

The Incident Management process started with the organisation's service desk (also known as the help desk). Either a user or customer would notice that something wasn't working as it should and would contact the service desk to report the issue and seek assistance. Incidents ranged from basic troubleshooting to major incidents that significantly disrupted IT services. The service desk consultant would raise a ticket in the service management software; identify, log, categorise, and prioritise the incident; and then attempt to triage or restore IT services to normal working levels.

If the incident required advanced support, the service desk consultant would inform the user or customer that their issue would need to be escalated and investigated. An automated ticket number would also be sent in an email to the person who reported the issue, so they could track progress. The service desk consultant would raise a new ticket and assign it to second-level specialists in the service management software. Based on categorisation, a predefined notification and escalation procedure would ensue.

The IT leaders were told by the service desk manager that over 45 per cent of tickets were resolved and closed by the service desk, 'one stop' (known internally as first contact resolution). When they dug a little deeper, the leaders learned that what one stop actually meant was 'We can't do anything further with it and have to pass it onto someone else'. When the leaders looked at how many tickets were *actually* completed by one stop, they found it was less than 10 per cent. Most tickets were either passed back to the customer or user for more information or handed off to second-level specialists.

The leaders had assumed that implementing a self-service portal for users and customers would reduce demand for the service desk; however, they learned the opposite was true. Demand had grown by 203 per cent. The IT leaders learned that the reason for the increase wasn't due to more incidents being raised; it was due to their current organisational systems and structures that caused high levels of failure demand into the service desk. (See chapter 11, Failure demand – The invisible expense.) A high proportion of demand was found to be customers and users who were restating that they were still unable to do what they needed to do with their IT services (which had already been logged) or were chasing a previously raised ticket. Each time progress was chased, a service desk consultant created a new ticket and sent it to level two again. A standard 'We are working on it' response was given to the person chasing. The consequence of the system design meant that, effectively, the service desk had, more often than not, just become an intermediary between the person who raised the incident and the second-level specialist.

The IT leaders went on to discover what happened to tickets that were escalated beyond the service desk. Working to service level agreements, a second-level specialist would pick up a ticket from their work queue. They were tasked to investigate the cause and possible solutions for each incident. They, too, would attempt to resolve each incident in their queue. The leaders learned that less than 15 per cent of incidents were resolved by level-two specialists. The majority of incidents required additional support from level-three specialists, such as Infrastructure, Security, Database Administration, and so on. Therefore, level-two specialists would complete their work, mark their tickets as closed, and then raise additional tickets for each level-three specialist required to resolve the incident.

What started as one ticket created by the service desk often ballooned into numerous other tickets passed onto other IT specialists. After collating this data and putting it into a control chart (see chapter 16, Are you running your organisation through the rear-view mirror?), the leaders found that it was typical and predictable for one ticket to create up to 20 additional tickets that were farmed out around various areas within the IT department. As a result, the leaders learned that over 60 per cent of the tickets in the service management software were raised by IT themselves to get other IT colleagues to do work.

When tickets were distributed to various specialist teams, the assumption was that all tickets would arrive in the right place, the people where the tickets arrived would have the right skills, that the work would be done in the standard times, and that all tickets would pop back out again, clean. This assumption was based on a reliance on digitised workflows in the newly purchased service management software. When the IT leaders studied their service, we asked them to see how many of the distributed tickets between teams came back as clean. The answer was none. They were amazed to see the extent of unproductive activity that resulted through chasing, reworking, and duplication, with tens of people involved.

Problems also arose when tickets arrived at the various level-three specialist queues but the people tasked with restoring services didn't have all the skills needed to resolve an incident. When they needed help from specialists who did have the required skill sets, these people were often busy working on project delivery tasks. The leaders learned that there was a strong mythology among project managers that each time specialists were pulled away from their project tasks to help deal with an incident, project timelines slipped, which had negative consequences on delivery dates and budgets.

In other words, there were two conflicting internal de facto purposes at play in the organisation. The de facto purpose for people supporting the IT services was to manage an incident, whereas the de facto purpose for people managing projects was to deliver projects on time. Sharing resources to deliver these two different purposes caused inevitable confusion, waste of effort, and even conflict. Power structures had developed because managers were overstepping their authority. The IT leaders saw that the underlying causes for these conflicts were that roles were unclear, and authority and accountability weren't clearly defined.

Leaders also asked people in the various teams how long it took to resolve an incident end to end – no one knew. They could only point to their own team's performance numbers, for example, the volume of calls, emails, and chats; the number of tickets closed by that team; the number of open tickets; and the number of service level breaches. When work was done to manually tie together tickets from different teams to establish true end-to-end times, it predictably took an average of three days, but could still take up to 11 days to resolve a critical incident, and over a year for lower priority incidents.

Once Incident Management actions were complete and IT services were restored, the incident was closed in the service management software, and a Problem task was created. The purpose of a Problem task was to identify the incident's root cause to prevent reoccurrence.

Problem Management was the responsibility of the manager of the service management office. IT leadership held her accountable for ensuring that the root cause of an incident was identified and rectified. However, Problem Management was regarded as low-priority work by those project managers whose resources were needed to complete these investigations. As was the case with the incident management process, project managers were focused on delivering projects on time. Their view was that taking time out of busy project-delivery schedules to work on root cause analysis was not a good investment of time and money. The thinking in the IT department was that it was better to resolve an incident and move on. What the IT leaders learned was that they were holding the manager of the service management office to account for something they didn't have the authority to impact. She had all the accountability, but none of the authority. As a result, problem tasks were logged in the service management software to gather dust and never be revisited.

The lack of root cause analysis had caused thousands of tickets to be automatically created daily by various robots that monitored IT services. Large TV screens adorned the walls where IT specialists were located. Each screen displayed hundreds of rows of alerts in a table. The IT leaders saw that most of these alerts were ignored. People had learned that if an alert was actioned, it would inevitably pop back up again the next day, so they felt it wasn't worth looking at them. Perplexed, the leaders turned their attention to the monitoring team. They had assumed that people in the monitoring team were accountable for monitoring the alerts. However, while the monitoring team *created* automatic alerts, they didn't *monitor* them, it was discovered. Monitoring was deemed the responsibility of other teams.

Adding to the issues the IT teams faced was a lack of clarity and agreement for the authority associated with each role. The inevitable result was people who predictably overstepped their authority. The use of power emerged in this organisation because making decisions beyond the limits of their authority was seen as the only way to get things done. The use of power was either inadvertent or deliberate, depending on the person or situation. In both cases, though, it had led to relationships within the IT department being built on poor foundations and resulted in poor operational outcomes.

As a result of their experiential learning process, we asked the IT leaders to reflect on the following:

1. Why is it like this?

2. What is the effect on users and customers?

3. How much is this costing the organisation?

The IT leaders had learned that their current organisational systems and structures were causing high levels of failure demand, lots of unproductive activity, excess and compressed layers of management, increased backlogs of work, and unneeded operational expense. They now understood first-hand why many customers and users had a negative view of the service.

They could now see that the implementation of best practice frameworks and top-rated service management software had not addressed the root causes of poor performance and had, instead, merely locked in inefficiencies and cost. They had learned that people implementing frameworks, digitising workflows, and configuring software had been focused on the technical domain, with little attention paid to the social domain. (See chapter 15, Turning intention into productive reality.)

HIDDEN IMPROVEMENT OPPORTUNITIES

The experiential learning process from both the customer and user perspectives had diagnosed significant and previously hidden improvement opportunities in how to better service customers and users, work more efficiently, reduce operating costs, and improve engagement. Therefore, the decision was taken to redesign both the organisational systems and structures so that when an incident occurred, resolution was a simple and seamless process.

A productive structure was designed and implemented. (See chapter 17, Designing productive structures.) As a result, excess managerial layers were removed, people at all levels gained a clearer understanding of what was expected of them, people were enabled to use their full capabilities in exercising judgement and discretion in roles that freed them to work productively (see chapter 15, Turning intention into productive reality), and a far more productive working environment was created, so that each person understood where each other's authority started and finished. (See the section It is better to build relationships based on authority rather than power, in chapter 17, page 195.) Existing organisational systems were diagnosed, redesigned, and implemented. (See chapter 14, Liberating people and organisations from stultifying systems.) Leaders worked to change and sustain culture by using three leadership tools: leadership behaviour, organisational system design, and symbols. (See chapter 18, A cure for that déjà vu feeling of cultural resistance.) As a result:

- 87 per cent of tickets were truly resolved at one stop, without requiring a handoff (previously, it was fewer than 10 per cent)

- turnaround times for incident resolution reduced by 67 per cent

- failure demand into the service desk reduced by 42 per cent

- service availability significantly increased

- operational expense reduced by 20 per cent

- when surveyed, both customers and users stated they were far more satisfied with the new service

CASE STUDY 3: HOME LOANS

Whenever we ask leaders how much research they do, the answer is always a lot. When we ask how much of that data is used, the predictable answer is not a lot. Why is that? In our experience, we have found that the data that comes back from the research is often too generic, or tells the leaders no more than what they already knew.

Take the example of a large financial services organisation whose diminishing share of the home loan market had been an ongoing problem. Leaders in the home loans division had engaged an external consultancy to conduct research to understand why. Weeks of research was undertaken, including conducting focus groups and analysing markets, demographics, competitive features, channel usage, and dropout rates. Following detailed analysis, solutions to improve market share were offered, such as suggested product offerings, ideas for advertising and pricing, and new sales and service models, with an outline of recommended next steps provided. It was a well presented package; however, fundamentally, there was nothing in the findings that the leaders didn't already know – it did not provide the leaders with any new insights, so they did not believe they were any further ahead in how to redress the issues they faced.

The home loans leadership contacted us for help. We could see that the analysis was missing a true understanding of what matters to customers. Rather than providing another analysis of the issues to the leaders, we worked with the leaders to help *them* take a customer's perspective and learn first-hand what was happening. Through an experiential exercise, they learnt what creates value for customers wanting a home loan by understanding their circumstances, needs, and issues, and how well the organisation's services were designed to deliver value. This new first-hand knowledge revealed:

- The typical and predictable customer demands placed on the home loans service, and how well their services were designed to deliver value for each of those demands

- The amount of unproductive activity (cost) inherent in the current organisational systems and structures, and, more importantly, the causes of these costs

- The impact the organisational systems and structures had on productive behaviour and activity

- How people experienced their work, their leader, and the home loans area

- Shared mythologies underpinning existing culture

The leaders studied three types of home loans:

- New Loans

- Refinance – where the value of a property has increased, and the customer wants to borrow more than the original loan, up to the new value of their property

- Redraw – where the customer wants to redraw some of the funds previously paid into their home loan

To understand typical and predictable demands placed on the home loans service and how well their services were designed to deliver value for each of those demands, the leaders went to the points of transaction where customers interacted with the organisation, namely, mortgage brokers, branches, and the contact centre.

When they visited mortgage brokers, the leaders found that brokers spent a lot of their time contacting the organisation to query issues, reply to issues, supply additional documentation, or chase the progress of applications on behalf of customers. A lot of hidden unproductive activity and cost was revealed, both for brokers and for the organisation.

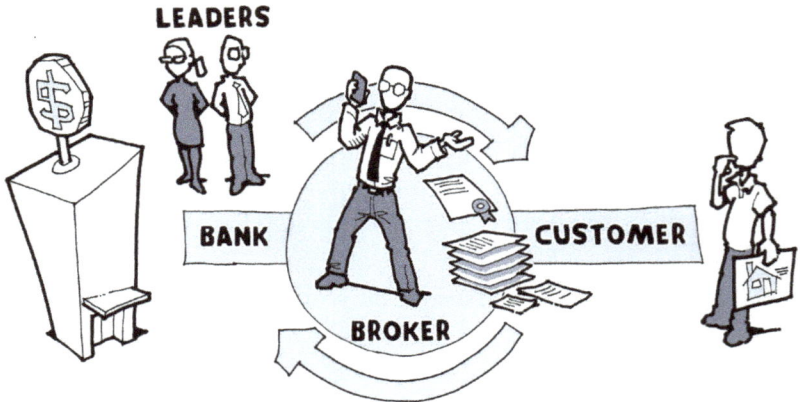

Next, the leaders visited branches. They observed customers enter a branch and take a ticket from a machine and wait in a queue (like a supermarket deli system). We suggested the leaders talk to those who had taken a ticket related to home loans and ascertain the following:

1. What problem does the customer want solved?

2. Is it our failure to do something, or to do something right?

3. How able are we to understand and deliver what they want, there and then?

The leaders began to understand that lots of customers who visited a branch were there because of failure demand. The leaders also learned that very little failure demand was dealt with at the branch. A decision had been made to reduce non-sales demand into branches. As a result, when presenting failure demand at a branch, customers were asked to either fill in a form, call the contact centre, or go online to resolve their problem. Forms and phone and internet booths had been provided in the branches for this purpose.

A decision had also been made to move mortgage applications to larger branches. The leaders visited several smaller branches to understand the impact. When potential customers visited a smaller branch to apply for a home loan and were told they would have to visit a larger branch, the leaders found that many of these potential customers decided it was easier to visit a local competitor instead. More hidden unproductive activity and cost had been revealed in the branches.

After visiting brokers and branches, the leaders spent time in the contact centre. They found that over 35 per cent of customer and broker demand into the contact centre that related to home loans was failure demand. The contact centre had effectively become a repair centre.

More hidden unproductive activity and cost had been revealed in the contact centre.

After learning what happens at the mortgage brokers, branches, and contact centre, we asked the leaders to follow home loan applications through the various functions involved in completing an application within the organisation, including back-office assessors, credit, pricing, property assessments, and so on. They found that in working to service level agreements and targets, each of these specialists picked up an application from their work queue, completed their portion of the work, then either passed it onto the next specialist or back to the previous specialist if there was a discrepancy.

The leaders learned that:

- There were over a hundred business rules in the process

- The same documentation was checked multiple times by different people

- Decisions were checked multiple times by different people

- When working on an application, people were required to record evidence of work into the mortgage software tool multiple times

- A high percentage of granted applications were reworked

- Nearly half of all applications in the previous year resulted in queries from customers

Hidden unproductive activity and cost had been revealed in the back-office functions too.

We asked the leaders to understand how long it took, end to end, for mortgage applications to be completed. This data was not readily available, as mortgage processing was separated by function, and the data was stored in different IT tools used by the various specialists. No one had a complete view. All that was available were measures of how each team performed against targets and SLAs and how busy people were. When work was done to manually calculate true end-to-end times for each home loan, it was found that:

- For new loans, the average time from application to decision took a week, and the average time from application to payment took almost three months

- For refinance, the average time from application to decision took over a week, and the average time from application to payment took over a month

- For redraw, the average time from application to decision took over a week, and the average from application to payment took a month

As a result of their experiential learning process, we asked the leaders to reflect on the following:

1. Why is it like this?

2. What would cause customers to go elsewhere?

3. How much is this costing the organisation?

The home-loan leaders learned that their current organisational systems and structures caused high levels of failure demand, lots of unproductive activity, increased backlogs of work, and unneeded operational expense. Most surprisingly, they learned that only a very small percentage of customers asking for a home loan ended up with a loan, because the process took too long. The leaders learned that despite millions being poured into advertising to attract customers, conversion rates were very low due to stultifying systems and structures. They now understood first-hand why many customers had a negative view of the service and chose to go elsewhere for their home loan.

**HIDDEN
IMPROVEMENT
OPPORTUNITIES**

The experiential learning process from the customer perspective had diagnosed significant and previously hidden improvement opportunities in how to better attract, acquire and service home-loan customers, work more efficiently, and reduce operating costs. Therefore, the decision was taken to redesign the organisational systems and structures to improve the service.

A productive structure was designed and implemented. (See chapter 17, Designing productive structures.) As a result, people at all levels gained a clearer understanding of what was expected of them, people were enabled to use their full capabilities in exercising judgement and discretion in roles that freed them to work productively (see chapter 15, Turning intention into productive reality), and a far more productive working environment was created, so each person understood where each other's authority started and finished. (See the section It is better to build relationships based on authority rather than power, in chapter 17, page 195.) Existing organisational systems were diagnosed, redesigned, and implemented. (See chapter 14, Liberating people and organisations from stultifying systems.) Leaders worked to change and sustain culture by using three leadership tools: leadership behaviour, organisational system design, and symbols. (See chapter 18, A cure for that déjà vu feeling of cultural resistance.)

Rather than having separate functions to pass work between each other to complete a home loan application, teams with the required skill sets were formed. Each team had the capability and authority to use judgement and discretion to complete the minimum required work, for example, application assessment, credit decisions, pricing, property assessments, and paying out of funds, without the need to pass on or delegate to anyone else. (See chapter 15, Turning intention into productive reality.)

Technologists worked alongside their front-line colleagues taking new home loan applications to understand what creates value for customers. This created a shared body of knowledge that related back to customers and the way customer work was done. The technologists were able to see first-hand that much of the organisation's IT tools were hindering their colleagues from creating value for customers. Many of the business rules in the process were embedded in the tools, and forced people to follow the process, no matter how unproductive some of the steps were. With this knowledge, the technologists could understand and identify where technology could complement human activity, rather than control it. The IT leaders focused on creating the capability so that when a productive organisational system was designed and implemented, the technology could change and adapt with it. Previously, several IT tools were required to make a credit decision. Technologists solved this problem by having all these IT tools operate in the background and, instead, created a single screen that would display the required information.

These are examples of the many changes that were adopted. The overall result was a transformed home loan service:

- New Loans – the average time from application to decision reduced by 43 per cent, and the average time from application to payment reduced by 63 per cent

- Refinance – the average time from application to decision was reduced from more than a week to being completed within the day, and the average time from application to payment reduced by 93 per cent

- Redraw – the average time from application to decision was reduced from more than a week to being completed within the day, and the average time from application to payment reduced from more than a month to being completed within the day

- Failure demand related to home loans greatly diminished

- Market share increased

The economics of these results are startling: more customers, reduced unproductive activity (cost), loan applications finalised sooner, thus receiving customer payments earlier, new business through word of mouth, and it was no longer necessary to choose between reducing costs and improving service.

CONCLUSION

We hope that what you have read in this book has caused you to pause and think, or rather, re-think, what you currently thought to be good practice to positively change your service organisation for the benefit of all.

In part one, we presented a collection of thought-provoking articles and essays on where the purpose of an organisation has been unintentionally undermined by misinformed leadership and unproductive organisation, resulting in negative experiences for customers and employees.

The articles and essays may have challenged your current view. However, throughout the book we have revealed the causes for the negative view of service organisations when seen through the lens of a customer and an employee, and why so much of the work that is done is unproductive.

Some of the arguments we have made, and the issues we have highlighted, may have resonated or disturbed. You are not alone. Progressive leaders are often frustrated by the way conventional organisations function and the consequences that result, frustration that is only compounded further by the inability of traditional change approaches, fads, and magic cures to create productive and positively viewed organisations that deliver lasting improvements in service delivery, leadership, and culture.

In part two, we offered a unique approach for creating an organisation that is positively viewed by customers and employees, and how to help people come together to achieve the purpose the organisation has been set up to accomplish. We described the practical methods and leadership tools to transform your organisation to give every customer exceptional service at less cost to the organisation, build leadership capability to enable people to work more productively, and create lasting positive change in people's behaviour and organisational culture.

The practical methods and leadership tools we described in part two are based upon a coherent and integrated theory of organisational behaviour about how to lead and organise service organisations, underpinned by over 25 years of research and application in the field. Through reconceiving and reconceptualising service delivery, leadership, and culture, private sector organisations have vastly improved customer satisfaction, retention, and sales; reduced operational expense; and improved employee engagement through creating an organisation that allows people to work productively, to their potential. Public sector and voluntary organisations have created far simpler and better experiences for each person using a service (often at a time of great need), and at the same time achieve far more under constrained budgets whilst creating a more productive and sustainable work environment.

It is rare nowadays to encounter a situation where an organisation is not already implementing, or planning to implement, organisational change initiatives. Typically, organisations pursue these initiatives for one or more reasons, such as to realise cost reductions, performance improvement, and/or customer satisfaction.

Our experience, however, is that each of these change initiatives tends to focus heavily on one specific area of work, for example, implementing technology, restructuring, or culture change, rather than providing an integrated and comprehensive approach to create and sustain change.

Although the operational changes may be specified in some detail, the impact on the people concerned, and their behaviour, is often underestimated or misunderstood. Since the required improvements will inevitably depend on people changing their behaviour, it is concerning that few initiatives are underpinned by a sound theoretical understanding of social process and human behaviour. A change initiative may describe, in some detail, *what* behaviours are required, but it is rare to find an explanation of *why* or *how* behaviours will change.

What we have described can strengthen any implementation by providing an overarching framework which is based on a sound theoretical understanding of human behaviour. This enables an accurate diagnosis of relevant past and current organisational issues. It also provides the opportunity to predict how behaviours might change in response to changes in organisational strategies, structures, systems, and new leadership behaviours.

Of course, there are many other approaches being used to understand and improve organisations. Our advice for anyone considering any approach is to start with a few questions:

1. Are you clear about your purpose?

2. Why have you chosen this approach? How does it relate to other planned or ongoing change initiatives?

3. Does the approach clearly explain why it should or should not work?

4. Is it based on sound theory? Is it predictive?

5. Where is the evidence?

6. How does it fit with the current systems and structures, and what might need to be changed?

7. Do you have the capability and determination to implement?

Likewise, you will have also found some interesting theory in this book, but, as we have pointed out previously, our advice is that it is always important to ask: *Would it work for you?* You may have also been thinking that if what we have proposed is so good, why isn't everyone already doing this? The answer to that is straightforward – it requires you, as a progressive leader, to question and challenge underlying assumptions and beliefs about human behaviour and how organisations should be set up, led, and organised.

As discussed in this book, many approaches to organisational effectiveness and design are really fads and/or rebadged techniques that are implemented because of 'best practice'. One year it's leadership, the next it's teamwork, the next it's collaboration, and the next (and current) it's new ways of working. It is attractive to think that one approach – promoted as a magic formula or silver bullet – will fix the problem. Of course these ideas have merit – clearly, all organisations need leadership and better ways of working, and it is self-evident that we cannot work together without teamwork and collaboration. However, what these terms actually mean and how they are interpreted and translated into action can vary significantly. We have seen many of these fads and trends come and go over the years, and whilst they seem appealing, unfortunately, they invariably result in disappointment. When we have examined each, we find that they do not have a strong theoretical base and are, thus predictably, short-lived.

We don't offer a magic formula or silver bullet. We appreciate that creating, sustaining, and improving an organisation is hard work. There is no way around that. We have found that it is incredibly worthwhile to spend the time at the beginning to work out the desired outcome(s) and why any approach might be expected to deliver these. That is the work of the leadership, and we have found that reconceiving service, leadership, and culture can not only help in that process but also help to understand what other approaches may or may not be complementary.

We have described an extremely effective way for you to understand and test your own assumptions and beliefs by looking at your organisation from a customer's perspective. Spend a few hours to see for yourself what happens where customers interact with your organisation, then repeat this process, but do so now from an employee's perspective. We know that you will be astonished when you realise the money wasted and damage inadvertently inflicted on your customers and brand. You will see first-hand how the systems designed into your organisation have driven unexpected behaviour, caused immense frustration, created excessive levels of unproductive activity and effort (cost), and hamstrung your colleagues from working effectively. Each and every leader we have worked with also knows that the good news is that you will quickly see the opportunity for improvement too, with stunning cost reductions and exceptional service delivery improvements suddenly visible.

As Albert Einstein said, 'We cannot solve our problems with the same thinking we used when we created them'. If your role in a service organisation is operational leadership, executive leadership, or as a board member, and you are frustrated by the way service organisations function and dissatisfied with the status quo; frustrated when it comes to delivering lasting improvements in work, leadership, and culture, compounded further by the inability of traditional change approaches, fads, and magic cures; someone who actually likes, respects, and is fascinated by people, and intuitively understands that leadership is about creating social cohesion; comfortable that your role is ever-changing rather than fixed, and that your role is to support, enable, and build capability in others to work productively, to their potential; are open to new ideas and receptive to change; and you are someone who still loves to learn, this book will have provided fresh thinking and opportunities on how to transform your organisation to give every customer exceptional service at less cost to the organisation. It will have provided valuable insights into how to build leadership capability to enable people to work more productively, and how to create lasting positive change in people's behaviour and organisational culture.

It is our aim with this book to have helped you, as a progressive leader, to positively change your service organisation for the benefit of all and that you are able to realise the following outcomes for you, your colleagues, your organisation and your customers:

- A true understanding of what creates value for your customers, through learning their circumstances, needs, and issues

- Deliver exceptional services by servicing your customers through the most effective means, wherever they interact with the organisation

- Vastly improved customer satisfaction, by getting it right for your customers the first time, through designing services that are adaptable and responsive

- Colleagues who are enabled to work more productively through working in a far better and more efficient organisational design

- Reduced operational expense and increased capacity after removing failure demand and unproductive activity (cost)

- Achieve far more under constrained budgets whilst creating a more productive and sustainable work environment

- Managers at all levels are able, and seen, to add value to their team members

- Technology that complements human activity, enhances cognitive processes, automates simple and repetitive tasks, and further improves productive work

- Social cohesion that enables people to work productively to their potential

- Clarity for everyone about what they do, how well they are working, as an individual and as part of a team, and how they work together

- Structures that recognise work complexity to ensure everyone works on the right work, has the right authority, the right capability, and demonstrates positive behaviour

- All working relationships, hierarchical and lateral, are clearly understood and productive

- A continual and systematic understanding of shared mythologies underpinning existing organisational culture through understanding how people experience their work, their leaders, their colleagues, and the organisation

- Formation of a productive culture at all levels, through every single interaction

- Leading measures that help leaders understand how well work achieves the purpose the organisation has been set up to accomplish

- Leaders that consistently use positive leadership behaviour and symbolism to create, maintain, and improve the culture of a group of people so that they achieve objectives and continue to do so over time

- Proof of economic benefit

Maybe the last word should go to two progressive leaders of organisations who adapted and adopted the theory, practical methods, and leadership tools described in this book.

Renato Mota, Chief Executive Officer of Insignia Financial:

    ❝ *We've been able to simplify how we think about our business, and we have greater confidence that it aligns to our customers, and we can measure that in a far more meaningful way. These are the things that now manage our business. We now get a very rich picture of what matters to a customer.*

    This has done more for staff satisfaction than anything else we have done in our organisation. Giving people a sense of purpose and giving them an ability to deliver value will do more for your people than anything else you will do. We've got better customer satisfaction, and more empowered and knowledgeable frontline staff, who are making quicker decisions and are delivering value more quickly.

    This learning and rethinking experience has led to a transformation in our strategy. The redesign of our system is giving us a significant advantage in our ability to deliver value.

Danik Lucas, an executive at WorkCover Queensland:

    ❝ *Through working with Reconceive, I learnt our organisation had some typical large organisational design principles and management assumptions strongly embedded in its operations. I've learned that these are sometimes the very things that constrain rather than enable organisations to do what matters to customers.*

    To better support our customers and deliver exceptional experiences every day, we learned that we needed to make a significant change to our systems and structures. We didn't just tweak processes. We weren't looking to make small changes or put Band-Aids over what we already had. Through this process, we understood that we had to redesign the organisational systems and structures from the ground up.

We rebuilt capability, rebuilt the organisational systems, and redefined roles. We totally changed the role of the leaders, clarified leadership at all levels, and conducted a significant restructure of our entire customer group.

In the redesigned systems, our frontline people have clarity about their work, can improve their own work, can use judgement and discretion, and receive real-time recognition. Because they get it right up front, they don't have to spend unproductive time dealing with failure demand during the day.

I'm really proud of the work that we've done to better support our customers. We learned that what mattered to our customers was a quick decision on their claim. We can now measure that directly in customer terms. By doing this, there is no doubt that we've delivered an improvement for customers. The feedback we've had is that our customers are amazed by the improved service.

The unique approach for transforming an organisation detailed in this book, has resulted in us being recognised by the Customer Service Institute of Australia who awarded us the 2021 'Customer Service Project of the Year' for continuous improvement.

ACKNOWLEDGEMENTS

We would like to recognise the work of John Seddon, the British organisational psychologist. Inspired by Deming's declaration that organisations should be managed as systems, and intervention theory – that changing thinking is the key to improvement – John developed the Vanguard Method. John's body of work, as described in the book *Beyond Command and Control*, has been central in how the authors have been able to help progressive leaders create productive and positively viewed organisations that give every customer exceptional service at less cost to the organisation.

Command-and-control management has created service organisations that are full of waste, offer poor service, depress the morale of those who work in them and are beset with management factories that not only do not contribute to improving the work, but actually make it worse. The management principles that have guided the development of these organisations are logical—but it's the wrong logic. (Seddon 2005)

We would also like to acknowledge the work completed by Ian Macdonald, Catherine Burke and Karl Stewart. Their body of work as described in the book *Systems Leadership: Creating Positive Organisations* has been central to how the authors have been able to help organisations build leadership capability to enable people to work productively and create lasting positive change in people's behaviour and organisational culture.

There are many different ideas, often fragmented, about how to lead, design and set up organisations. They are often short-term "initiatives", subject to fads or flavours of the month. Such ideas often come and go or only cover one aspect. They may assume that the answer is in one or two activities, such as "leadership", "collaboration", "empowerment", "creativity", "innovation" and so on. Such approaches can be well intentioned but can be vague as to the "how" and certainly unclear as to what behaviour change is expected or what new systems and structures need to be implemented to underpin any change. As a result there can be significant variation in approach and results but without a clear understanding of what actually works well and why. Systems Leadership is a comprehensive and coherent framework, which provides concepts, models and tools for leaders and managers in organisations to use in their work to improve the working lives of people and hence the effectiveness of their organisation. It actually provides a predictive model as to what works well according the context. In short, it gives you the benefit of foresight. (Macdonald, Burke and Stewart 2018)

Embedded in this book are concepts and work undertaken by these authors. We have not referenced every occurrence individually, for ease of reading, but wish to acknowledge here that we've made use of material from their work without specific acknowledgement on each occasion.

We'd also like to recognise the work of others who have contributed to the theory, practical methods, and leadership tools contained in the book: Dr Elliott Jaques and Wilfred Brown: 'Stratified systems theory'; Chris Argyris: 'Double loop learning theory' and 'Intervention theory and method'; W. Edwards Deming: 'Theory of profound knowledge'; Genichi Taguchi: 'Loss function'; and Walter A. Shewhart: 'Theory of variation and statistical process control'.

Additionally, we'd like to thank Roger Harvey for creating the amazing illustrations and cartoons used throughout this book; these have helped enormously in bringing this book to life.

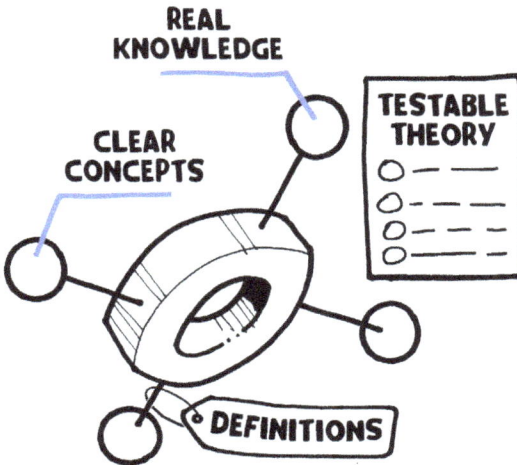

GLOSSARY

Accountability: A component of a work relationship between two people wherein an individual can be called to account for their actions by another individual or body authorised by both parties. The critical part of this statement is 'authorised by both parties'.

Activity Management: Managers of service organisations predominantly manage using the following equation: 'How much work have we got?', 'How long does it take to do the work?', and 'How many people do I need to do the work?' These three questions drive managerial decision making, leading managers to become fixated on managing people's activity – how many things they did, how long it took them to do each task, what was in their queue, and so on. This often creates a burgeoning and bureaucratic measurement system with a focus on the activity at the expense of achievement of purpose. Employees are then regularly monitored and surveilled using technology, so activity can be measured.

Arbitrary Measures: Typically, what is measured are things that leaders will have judged and assumed to be important; for example, performance targets, budgets, work states, service levels, activity, objectives, incentives and so on. We classify these as arbitrary measures, that is, a standard that someone has arbitrarily set as a measure of success or failure.

Authority: The right, given by constitution, law, role description, or mutual agreement for one person to require another person to act in a prescribed way (specified in the document or agreement). The likelihood of exercising authority effectively usually depends upon good social process skills and the application of action in the context of the mutual acceptance of agreed limits. It is essential that there is a clear understanding of the difference between authority and power (see below), and that authority is not a one-way process.

Authority and Power: Person A has authority or power in relation to person B when person A is able to have person B behave as A directs. If person B does not so behave, neither authority nor power has been exercised. Authority applies within the boundary and constraints of the law, policy, and rules of the organisation and those of accepted social custom and practice. Power breaches one or more of these constraints to authority.

Capability: Knowledge; technical skills; social process skills; mental processing ability; application (desire, energy, and drive applied to work).

Contingent Relationship: A relationship where 'If you do this, then you get that'. This type of relationship causes the person to focus on the 'you get that', rather than achieving the purpose the organisation has been set up to accomplish.

Control Chart: Understanding variation helps managers to learn what to expect. Walter Shewhart created what are called control charts. He showed that, using a basic statistical formula, people can see whether variation is predictable or unpredictable. Control charts can be used to measure the variation, or predictability, of what it feels like for customers who use a service.

Control Limits: Used in a control chart. The upper and lower control limits (UCL and LCL) are calculated from the variation between the series of data points in a control chart. If all data is between the UCL and LCL, your system is in control and performance is predictable.

Critical Issue: Something that, if not satisfactorily resolved, threatens the achievement of the purpose of the work of an individual, team, or organisation.

Culture: A culture is a group of people who share a common set of mythologies. The group may be very large or relatively small and the strength of the culture will be determined by the number of mythologies that are common to the group. It is normal for there to be smaller common interest groups within a large cultural group and these are often referred to as subcultures. The commonality of the mythologies causes all the members of a culture to ascribe the same value assessment to a system, symbol, or behaviour that they experience, regardless of whether that assessment is positive or negative.

Customer: The people that an organisation works together to serve, without which the service would not need to exist. The term customer could also be known as user, consumer, or citizen.

De Facto Purpose: Rather than starting with a purpose defined from the intent of an organisation, it is a common error to create a de facto purpose that drives behaviour, e.g. 'make the numbers'.

Demand: Transactional services are ones where customers place demands on the service organisation, and represent the vast majority of services. There are only two groups of demands that come from customers: value demand and failure demand. With thorough knowledge of demand, we can design exceptional services that work for customers and cost less.

Dissonance: An experience where our expectations or predictions are challenged. Often, the experience of dissonance is profound. People experience a state of mind generated by the clear failure of a prediction that has been based upon a strongly held belief. This is a challenge, major or minor, to our worldview. Dissonance is at the heart of all behaviour change. Dissonance need not always be negative. The positive aspect of a shift of balance can be summed up in the phrase 'the penny dropped', or 'the light went on'.

Exceptional Customer Service (creating value for customers): Delivering exceptional customer experiences and creating value for customers requires meeting the customers' nominal value.

Failure Demand: A failure to do something, or do something right, for customers. As much as 80 per cent of demand placed on a service organisation by customers can be failure demand. Until leaders learn to see failure demand and, more importantly, eliminate it once its root cause is identified and fixed, it is an invisible problem. Failure demand stands in contrast to value demand.

Hierarchy: An organisational structure wherein the authority available to a role increases upwards through the structure, increasing as work complexity increases. The authority structure of the organisation is made visible and accessible by means of role titles. In a correctly structured organisation, each role has the authority that is necessary to perform the work assigned to the role and this provides the connection between role authority and work.

Lagging Measures: Customer satisfaction, staff morale, and all financial measures are examples of lagging measures. Whilst these are not arbitrary measures, lagging measures can only tell managers what has happened, and will never help them understand why.

Leader: A leader is a person who demonstrates the exercise of power or authority, or both, and causes a group of people to act in concert to achieve a purpose. The objective of a correctly functioning organisation is to have all of its leaders clearly identified and exercising authority for the effective and efficient achievement of the purpose of the organisation and where that authority is willingly accepted. Within an employment hierarchy, all managers are leaders, but not all leaders are managers.

Leader, Work of: The work of a leader is to create, maintain, and improve the culture of a group of people so that they achieve objectives and continue to do so over time. Leaders can work to change and sustain the culture that they desire by using three leadership tools: leadership behaviour (what we do and say), organisational system design (how we do things), and symbols (non-verbal messages of what we do and how we do it). Importantly, these leadership tools need to be used consistently and persistently, with coherence and without contradiction.

Leading Measures: Leading measures help leaders understand how well work achieves the purpose the organisation has been set up to accomplish.

Levels of Work: The sequence of qualitatively different complexity pathways that need to be created to achieve goals when performing work. Depending upon the inherent complexity of a particular task, it will only be completed successfully if that complexity is resolved; hence, it falls into a specific level of work.

Management: The work of ordering and sequencing the application of resources to achieve a predetermined purpose. Good management does this effectively and efficiently. Human capability, in all its aspects, is one of the resources available to a manager that needs to be applied through person-to-person interaction.

Manager: A person who is accountable for their work and the work performance of others, such as a team. Managers are leaders because every manager is accountable for the leadership they provide to those who work for them. Within an employment hierarchy, all managers are leaders, but not all leaders are managers.

Mental Processing Ability (MPA): The ability of a person to generate order from the chaos by means of thought. The generation of order, which requires the understanding of relationships, is essential if intention is to be turned into reality, i.e., work is done. It is the ability to make order out of the chaotic environment in which humans live out their lives and in which they work. It is the ability to pattern and construe the world in terms of scale and time. The level of our MPA will determine the amount and complexity of information that we can process in doing so. Not all people have the same ability to generate order (MPA) and, hence, the same ability to perform work. Some will be able to resolve more complex problems than others.

Mythology: From Mythos, the story with emotional content, and Logos, the explanatory rationale or meaning of the story. Our mythologies are our beliefs about whether what we see strengthens social cohesion in our group or weakens it. Mythologies are not changed; new ones need to be constructed. Mythologies may lie dormant for years and can be enlivened by a future event. The process of changing or creating a culture requires the generation of new mythologies that are common to the group. We look at systems, symbols, and people's behaviour through the lens of our mythologies and assign what we see to a place on one or more of the scales of human values.

Nominal Value (what matters): In service, it's the customer who sets the nominal value. If the service organisation understands a customer's circumstances, needs, and issues, and responds to what matters to them (their nominal value), they have an exceptional customer experience and value is delivered. If the experience is poor, and the service does not give customers what they want, and in the way they want it (their nominal value), then the cost of service rises.

Organisational Level: A band across an organisation in which all the roles have a similar distribution of work complexity (level of work).

Organisational Structure: The arrangement of the roles in an organisation that, when correctly done, identifies and matches work complexity and the authority necessary to perform that work so the purpose of the organisation is achieved efficiently and effectively over time. The structure is the equivalent of the skeleton of the organisation; typically, its form is made visible and accessible through organisational charts.

Power: What is exhibited by a person who makes decisions beyond the limits of their authority.

Productive Activity: Activity that directly contributes to meeting the purpose the organisation has been set up to achieve.

Purpose (of a service): The reason the service exists from a customer's perspective.

Responsibility: Synonymous with accountability, but its long use in organisations that failed to hold people responsible has led to its general use as a collective noun for tasks, as in, 'your responsibilities are as follows…', 'the general responsibilities of the role are…', etc.

Service Capability: How well the service achieves purpose, measured in terms that matter to customers, e.g., timeliness, getting it right the first time.

Service Capacity: The measure of demand entering the service, e.g., the number of phone calls received by the call centre each day.

Social Process: Person-to-person interaction wherein the behaviour of each has a bearing upon the thoughts, emotions, and behaviour of the other.

Social Process Skills: Social process skills are those skills that give the ability to observe social behaviour, comprehend the embedded social information, and respond in a way that influences subsequent behaviour in a predictable way. In an organisation, this results in behaviour that contributes to the purpose of the organisation.

Symbol: The outward manifestation of a cultural group, e.g., flags, rituals, medals, posters, slogans. Symbols can be used by all leaders but become more significant as the organisational distance increases between the leader and the employees or team members.

System: A system is a framework that orders and sequences activity within the organisation to achieve a purpose. Systems are the organisational equivalent of behaviour in human interaction. Systems are the means by which organisations put policies into action. It is the owner of a system who has the authority to change it.

System Owner: The role within the organisation that authorises the purpose of the system and its design and implementation to achieve that purpose.

Systems of Differentiation: Systems that treat people differently, e.g., remuneration systems based on work performance.

Systems of Equalisation: Systems that treat people the same, irrespective of organisational criteria, e.g., safety systems.

Systems Leadership: An internally coherent and integrated theory of organisational behaviour. It is a body of knowledge that helps not only to understand why people behave the way they do but also, and perhaps more importantly, predict the way that people are likely to behave in organisations. Systems Leadership is essentially about how to create, improve, and sustain successful organisations.

Team: A team is a group of people, including a leader, with a common purpose who must interact with each other in order to perform their individual tasks and achieve their common purpose.

Teamwork: A team member is part of the whole. It is only by active co-operation, however, that the whole will be greater than the sum of the parts. The work of interaction that needs to be done by each team member promotes efficient and effective team functioning.

The Theory of Variation: To move beyond the limitations of normal practice, the theory of variation helps a leader to understand the concept of service capability and service capacity and recognise its implications for performance management. 1) We should expect things to vary; they always do. 2) Understanding variation will tell us what to expect. 3) Understanding variation leads to improvement. 4) Understanding variation tells us when there has been a genuine change in performance.

Time Span: The completion time of the longest task in a role equals the time span of the role. Time span is the elapsed time to disorder, effectively how long a person of a given capability is able to generate order in the chaos in which they are working.

Universal Values: A typology of six universal human experiences that rate or judge all behaviours, systems, and symbols heuristically. Behaviours, systems, and symbols that are demonstrated and rated positively create social cohesion; those that are demonstrated negatively destroy it. There are six values. Each value describes a behaviour: loving, trustworthy, respectful, courageous, honest, fair.

Unproductive Activity (waste): Any activity that does not directly contribute to meeting the purpose the organisation has been set up to achieve.

Value Demand: The things customers want that the service exists to provide. Value demand stands in contrast to failure demand (a failure to do something, or do something right, for customers).

Vanguard Method: The Vanguard Method provides the means to study service organisations as systems. The knowledge this generates leads to informed choices for redesigning the organisation as a system. It gives leaders the means to change from a command-and-control design to a systems design.

Work: Turning intention into reality. The work required to create a successful organisation can be categorised into three distinct domains: a technical domain, which reflects activity relating to the knowledge and skills that are applied to tasks that help achieve the purpose of an organisation; a commercial domain, which can be described as the activity relating to costs, revenue, and capital – in short, value for money; and a social domain, which consists of all the activity needed to allow people to work together.